Wanted: World Christians

Wanted:
World Christians

J. Herbert Kane

BAKER BOOK HOUSE
Grand Rapids, Michigan 49506

To
Ralph D. Winter
foremost missionary thinker
dynamic missionary activist
and
World Christian par excellence

77318

Contents

Foreword

"His ability to communicate in Chinese, and especially his practice of writing his own letters in Chinese script"—this is what impressed Arthur Glasser when he first met Herb Kane in China, back in the late 1930s.

How could God pull back from the field a superbly adapted missionary like that? Well, God had unexpected things for China too, as Communism shouldered responsibility for the largest human bloc in the world.

God certainly did have significant plans for Herbert Kane. The years in China (1935–50) were only an intense, superb prologue to a long life of amazing productivity and blessing.

No one in United States history has ever produced a wider range of basic texts on the Christian mission. No mission leader, I know, has had such a close brush with cancer and suffered seven ministrokes in one week, and survived for further vital service. And he has never stopped thinking—or working.

No one, I know, has covered more ground in the classroom, over more years, with as much balance and detail, with as great a gift for pungent insight and friendly humor. Here is a man who combines strong personal convictions with an amazing ability to hear what others are saying. He is really one of a kind.

And this book, so worth pondering chapter after chap-

ter—no light fluff here—runs the gamut of his practical,
well-informed, globe-girdling, biblical, hard-hitting writing at its best.

But this is no light novel. As you read on, you will be
brought alternately to tears and torment. What an incredibly complex world he grapples with, unflinchingly
taking on topics many would sooner avoid.

For example, Kane battles the critics of "triumphalism," who insist on hopelessness. He does so with a
fundamental optimism that shines through even his sobering treatment of the most serious problems of the
world.

Or, take the contrast: With a burgeoning world population more than twenty times as large as it was in Paul's
day, it is stupefying how many more people there are to
win today. Yet, the number of evangelical Bible-believing
Christians is greater than the entire world population in
Paul's day. This book guides you through many such perplexing paradoxes, with an earnest and steady hand.

How indebted we are to Herb Kane. *Wanted: World
Christians* is only his latest, eloquent contribution to students, pastors, Sunday-school teachers—all those whose
unreserved hearts for God allow them the great privilege
and challenge of being World Christians in today's world.

What a privilege to recommend it, unreservedly.

Ralph D. Winter
Director, U.S. Center for World Mission
Pasadena, California

T he concept of the World Christian is an idea whose time has come. In the past we took for granted that the evangelization of the world was the responsibility of a special group of people with a missionary "call." Everyone else was content to remain at home and "support" missions in a rather desultory fashion with their gifts, and sometimes with their prayers. Few church members regarded missionary work, at home or overseas, as a live option. There was little or no real, personal involvement.

All that is beginning to change, and the change is due to a number of diverse factors. Several major events in recent history have made the American people painfully aware of the world beyond our shores. World War II, the Korean War, and the Vietnam War suddenly sent Americans scurrying for their atlases to locate such exotic places as Al-Alamein, Rabaul, Midway, New Guinea, Saipan, Okinawa, the Yalu River, the Burma Road, and Heartbreak Ridge, not to mention Hiroshima and Nagasaki. Isolation, as a foreign policy, has been shattered at least for the foreseeable future. America can no longer shirk her responsibilities as a first-rate world power.

A second factor was the Peace Corps, launched by John F. Kennedy in 1960. That noble experiment convinced us that Americans can serve overseas in peace as well as in war. In 25 years some 120,000 volunteers have served in 90 countries; and when they returned, they shared their insights, experiences, and enthusiasm with the folks at home. As a result, the American people have come to realize that world service is not confined to a select few with special qualifications. Anyone between the ages of 18 to 80, provided he or she has a skill, can make a solid contribution to the development of Third World countries.

A third factor has been the appeal and outreach of such Christian youth groups as Youth With A Mission, Teen Missions, Operation Mobilization, and others. At the university level are such groups as Campus Crusade for Christ, Inter-Varsity Christian Fellowship, and the Navigators. Through these agencies tens of thousands of dedicated young people have been exposed to cross-cultural missionary work. Almost to a man, they have returned home all fired up about world missions, and their enthusiasm has rubbed off on their fellow students. They have had a taste of life on the mission field and will never be the same again. Even if they never become missionaries in the technical sense of the word, they have forever shed their provincialism. From now on, they will always think, plan, and pray in global terms.

If there is one person, above others, who has promoted the idea of the World Christian, it is Ralph D. Winter, director of the U.S. Center for World Mission in Pasadena, California. As an initiator, he is without a peer. He has started more missionary agencies than any living person; all of them are viable operations today. If Ralph Winter did not invent the term *World Christian,* he has certainly done more than anyone else to promote and popularize it.

His longest-standing preoccupation has to do with an estimated 17,000 "Hidden Peoples" all over the world that are beyond the reach of any existing church and can be reached only by cross-cultural missions. It is uncanny the way that Winter has captured the minds of Christian students all over the country. Everybody, it would appear, is talking about "Hidden Peoples" and thousands are giving serious consideration to cross-cultural missions, if only on a short-term basis. Obviously, God is doing a new thing in our day, and we cannot but praise Him for the widespread interest on the part of students in the world mission of the church.

This book is sent forth with the hope and prayer that it might be used of God to convince American Christians that the prime function of the church, between Pentecost and the Second Coming, is witness not worship, evangelism not exhortation; and that the responsibility for worldwide witness rests not on a chosen few, but on the Christian community as a whole. Not everyone can live and work abroad; but everyone *can* be a World Christian.

I wish to acknowledge a debt of gratitude to my son, G. Stanley Kane, professor of philosophy at Miami University, Oxford, Ohio, for his patient, careful, painstaking reading of the manuscript. His suggestions, additions, and deletions have been invaluable. Indeed, without his help, this book would never have seen the light of day.

J. Herbert Kane
Professor Emeritus
Trinity Evangelical
Divinity School
Deerfield, Illinois

PART I

An Introduction
The Basis for World Missions

What in the World Is God Doing?

The prevailing mood today is one of pessimism. The prophets of doom are everywhere, warning us of the approaching nuclear holocaust that could bring an end to civilization. The day of empire is over. The white man is on the run. The United Nation's deliberations are dominated by Third World countries, most of which are hostile to the political and economic systems in the West. Democracy has been tried and found wanting, and one by one the former colonies in Asia and Africa have settled for dictatorships which come and go with distressing frequency.

The Places God Is at Work

The Home Front

At home, the situation isn't much better. The whole fabric of American society is disintegrating. Our large cities seem unable to cope with such problems as unemployment, transportation, pollution, and vandalism. Divorce, drugs, adultery, and abortion have played havoc with the family. Our public school system is a disgrace to Western civilization. Our courts are clogged with lawsuits. Our prisons are bursting at the seams. In spite of record harvests, poverty and hunger are on the increase. Not too long ago, the theologians, of all people, were telling us that God is dead.

Well, God is not dead. He is very much alive. Moreover, He is still in control of the world and has not abandoned His plan one day to redeem the world. To this end He is actively at work in the worldwide missionary movement of our day.

We can be thankful that, in spite of the moral decadence in our country, God has not forsaken us. He is quietly going about the task of renewing His church. Church membership in the United States now stands at about 63 percent of the population—an all-time high. Church attendance among Catholics is 61 percent and among Protestants 39 percent. This compares very favorably with church attendance in the United Kingdom and the Continent, where church attendance is extremely low—in some countries less than 5 percent. Year after year the Bible continues to be the best seller. Christian radio and television stations proclaim the gospel each week to tens of millions of people, many of whom seldom attend church. Bible-study groups are to be found all over the country—in homes, in churches, in places of business, on university campuses, even in the halls of Congress.

The Third World

But if we want to see church growth at its best, we must go to the Third World. The modern missionary movement is barely two hundred years old. During the nineteenth century the going was difficult. Robert Morrison in China and Adoniram Judson in Burma both waited 7 years for the first convert to come forward for baptism. In Thailand it took the Presbyterians 19 years before they won the first Thai to faith in Christ. In other parts of the world the story was the same. Had it not been for the faith, patience, and perseverance of the early missionaries the mission might have been aborted before it got started.

That was the nineteenth century. Today we are in the last quarter of the twentieth century, and the situation is quite different. Everywhere God is at work, building His church, in His own way, by His own power, for His own glory. According to George Peters, as far as the Third World is concerned, "this is the day of salvation."

Never before in history have the non-Christian peoples of the world been so open to the claims of Christ. Millions, in all walks of life, are showing an unprecedented interest in the Christian faith. Animists in Africa, Hindus in India, Buddhists in Southeast Asia, Muslims in the Middle East are reading Christian literature, listening to gospel broadcasts, and enrolling in Bible correspondence courses in record numbers. Everywhere the Holy Spirit is at work, creating a hunger for the Bread of Life. And this quest for spiritual reality is not confined to the poor and the oppressed whose interest in religion might be suspect. This quest includes students in the universities, government personnel, military officers, professional and business people.

The newer churches in the Third World, with few exceptions, are throbbing with vigor and vitality. Missionaries on furlough are using two adjectives, "fabulous" and "fantastic," to describe the situation, and they are not exaggerating. Recently a missionary back from Hong Kong reported that the churches there are vibrant with young life. He mentioned one church, packed to the doors every week, where only 10 or 12 members are over 35 years of age!

After his return from a crusade in Korea in June 1973, Billy Graham said, "After what I have seen in Korea, my ministry will never be the same again." And he went on to add, "It may be that the center of spiritual gravity is shifting from the West to the East." Myron Augsburger, the well-known Mennonite radio preacher, upon his return from a tour of the mission fields of the world, said, "The cutting edge of the Christian church today is out there in the Third World."

Indeed it is. So succesful has missionary work been that in some cases the "daughter" churches established on the mission field are now larger than the "mother" churches in the West. The Christian and Missionary Alliance has more church members in Indonesia than here in the United States. The same is true of the Assemblies of God. They have a membership of around one million in the States, whereas in Latin America they have a community of ten million.

India

India, with the second largest population in the world, has yielded only a small number of converts. After five hundred years of Roman Catholic missions and two hundred years of Protestant missions, less than 4 percent of the population is Christian, and that includes everyone who calls himself a Christian, whether Catholic, Orthodox, or Protestant. The vast majority of the converts in the nineteenth century came from a background of "untouchability." Even today, some 60 percent of all church members are former low-caste Hindus. But that is changing.

In recent years the number of converts has been increasing. For the first 40 years the OMS International was able to establish only 1 church per year. Since 1980 that same mission has been planting 26 churches every year. In February 1982, Akbar Abdul-Haqq preached to 250,000 people in four campaigns in four cities. All over India there appears to be a new interest in Christianity, and among the converts are high-caste Hindus.

Korea

And what shall we say about Korea where church growth has been described as an "explosion"? In 1984, the churches celebrated the hundredth anniversary of the arrival of the first Protestant missionaries, Horace Underwood and Henry Appenzeller. And they had a lot to celebrate! If the present pattern of church growth continues, Korea may well become, by the year 2000, the only predominantly Protestant country in Asia.

The largest Methodist church in the world is the Kwang Lim Methodist Church in Seoul. The largest Presbyterian church is the Young Nak Presbyterian Church, also in Seoul. It has 65,000 members. If you think that is a large church, you ought to visit the Yoido Full Gospel Church with more than 500,000 members. To accommodate the crowd, it has seven services, back to back, every Sunday, and no one is permitted to attend more than one service!

Prior to partition along the thirty-eighth parallel in 1945, the majority of Christians were located in what is now North Korea. Since the destruction of the church by the Communists there, the largest concentration is in South Korea. There the churches are growing by leaps and bounds. In March 1979, there were 2,050 churches in Seoul. Thirty months later the number had soared to 4,700. Today the figure is close to 6,000.

Nor is church growth confined to the city of Seoul. It is estimated that six new churches are springing up in Korea every day. In January 1976, the Hap-Tong Presbyterian denomination had 2,484 churches. Three years later it had 3,884; and the growth continues.

The '80 World Evangelization Crusade, sponsored by Campus Crusade for Christ and known as "Here's Life, Korea," attracted a total attendance of 16,350,000 over a ten-day period. All-night prayer meetings were attended by 5,200,000 and 300,000 were given systematic training in evangelism. At the final rally more than 1,000,000 responded to a call to support home and foreign missions with their gifts and prayers. Some 300,000 volunteered to give one year to missionary service overseas.[1]

China

And if the growth in Korea is remarkable, the situation in China is even more startling. When the missionaries

---

1. Anyone interested in the church in Korea will want to read *Korean Church Growth Explosion*, ed. Ro Bong-Rin and Marlin L. Nelson (Seoul: Word of Life Press, 1983).

were obliged to leave in the early 1950s, total church membership was just below the one-million mark. The missionaries knew it was the end of the mission. They feared it would prove to be the end of the church as well, and the Great Proletarian Cultural Revolution (1966–69) seemed to confirm their worst fears. But the church did not die. It survived and grew at an amazing rate in recent years.

With the death of Mao Zedong and the rise to power of Deng Xiaoping in 1976, China turned her face once again toward the West, and we began to hear rumors of house churches springing up all over the country. The rumors, we feared, were too good to be true. There could not be *that* many Christians in China! Well, we were mistaken. Now we are told on good authority that there may be 50 million Christians in China. If that seems like an inflated figure, you can slice it in half and still have 25 million! If that figure is accurate, it represents the largest influx of new believers into the Christian church, by confession of faith, any time, anywhere, in two thousand years of church history. It is the Lord's doing and it is marvelous in our eyes.

The Chinese Communists made one fatal mistake. When they got rid of the missionaries, they forgot to include God! He remained after the missionaries left. And during the intervening years, our sovereign Lord has been working all things after the counsel of His own will and the result is astounding. Without missionaries, without Bibles, without hymnbooks, without pastors, and without church buildings, the Christians have multiplied thirty-, forty-, and fifty-fold in the past 35 years. Leslie Lyall's *God Reigns in China* makes exciting reading. So does David Adeney's *China: The Church's Long March*.

The Philippines

In recent years the Philippines has proved to be a very responsive field. Following the mass evacuation of China in the early 1950s a number of missions transferred their workers from China to the Philippines. As a result, church growth has experienced a veritable explosion. In 1970, the

All-Filipino Congress on Evangelism called for the formation of ten thousand evangelistic Bible-study groups in ten years. By 1973, that goal had been achieved. Then in 1980, some five hundred evangelical leaders from 81 denominations convened a Congress on Discipling a Nation. At the close of the congress they called for the formation of an evangelical church in every barrio by the year 2000. That would mean an increase from 10,000 to 50,000, and they have every reason to believe they will achieve their goal.

Burma

Burma is another case where the church has thrived without the presence of missionaries. All Protestant missionaries were expelled from Burma in 1966, but the work goes on and the churches continue to thrive. At Christmas in 1977, the tribal churches in the north got together to celebrate the hundredth anniversary of the coming of the gospel to that part of Burma. Christians, from all over the countryside, some 90,000 strong, gathered for ten days of celebration. Many of them traveled on foot, three and four days over mountains and through the jungles, bringing their meager supplies with them. For ten days they sang, prayed, and studied the Word together. During the celebration some six thousand persons were baptized. At the close of the meeting three hundred young people responded to a call to give two years to home missionary work. After 40 days of training, they were sent out. One mission agency supports eight hundred missionaries.

Black Africa

The situation in Black Africa is equally thrilling. More converts have been won to Christ in Africa than in all the other mission fields combined. In the early years, the going was hard and missionaries died like flies after the first frost. This was especially true in West Africa which came to be known as the "white man's grave."

But in the twentieth century, especially since World War II, church growth has experienced a quantum leap.

Today approximately half of Black Africa is Christian, with the Roman Catholics slightly outnumbering the Protestants. The fastest-growing group is the Independent, or Separatist, churches. If the present rate of growth continues, Africa in the twenty-first century may well be the most Christianized of all the continents.

One of my former colleagues at Trinity Evangelical Divinity School, Arthur P. Johnston, spoke one Sunday morning in a Baptist church in Bangui, capital of the Central African Republic. The church was packed, with people standing in the aisles and at the back of the church. When he was finished, Johnston sat down; whereupon the African pastor said to him, "Aren't you going to give an invitation?"

Johnston replied, "I didn't know I was expected to give an invitation. I didn't preach an evangelistic message."

"Oh," said the pastor, "in this church we give an invitation at every service."

"Well then," said Johnston, "perhaps you should give the invitation. You know your people better than I do."

Whereupon the pastor stood up and gave an invitation, and two hundred people pressed forward to accept Christ!

In 1982 evangelist Howard Jones conducted meetings in Africa. In Kinshasa total attendance reached 60,000, with three thousand decisions for Christ. In Gabon the press, radio, and television gave Jones extended coverage.

When the Christian and Missionary Alliance Church in Zaire celebrated its hundredth anniversary in 1984, some 25,000 Christians gathered in Bomo for a six-hour service. In addition to church and mission leaders, national dignitaries also graced the occasion with their presence: the Commissioner of Justice, representing the president; the Governor of Lower Zaire, the commissioner for the region; and the president of the Church of Christ in Zaire—an ecumenical body of which all the Protestant groups are "communities."

Until 1975 there was not a single church among the Maguzawa in Nigeria. Today there are 110 churches. In

1982, Bishop Festo Kivengere reported that church growth in Uganda was so rapid that he could not tell how many local congregations the Anglican Church had. "We are growing too fast," he said, "to keep this kind of record." In his own diocese the growth has been so rapid that the diocese was divided in two. He reported, "We now have 60 parishes, 600 churches, and 120 full-time pastors. Each church is expected to spawn two other churches in 1982."

All over Nigeria, the most populous country in Africa, the story is the same. The SIM-related churches have doubled in number every ten years since 1945, resulting in more than two thousand churches today.

Latin America

Latin America is another area of the world where God is at work. At the turn of the century there were approximately 50,000 Protestants (called Evangelicals) in Latin America. By 1950 the figure had risen to 5 million. Today the number is closer to 30 million. It is estimated that the number of Evangelicals in that part of the world is increasing about 10 percent per year. In Guatemala they now account for almost 25 percent of the population.

The Pentecostals are the ones in Latin America experiencing the greatest degree of church growth. And the growth continues without any sign of slackening. One reason for their rapid growth rate is their high visibility. C. Peter Wagner writes:

> The Christians there [in Chile] regularly move right into the streets to preach the gospel in the plazas and on street corners. In evenings and on weekends you can't walk far around the city of Santiago without running into a group of Pentecostals playing accordions, singing at the top of their lungs, and sharing testimony of their faith with whoever will listen. A large number of Christians trace their spiritual pilgrimage back to hearing the gospel preached out in the open air.[2]

---

2. C. Peter Wagner, *On the Crest of the Wave: Becoming a World Christian* (Ventura, Calif.: Regal, 1983), p. 22.

Wagner goes on to describe one of his "favorite" churches—the Jotabeche Methodist Pentecostal Church in Santiago. When they outgrew a 5,000-seat auditorium, they built one with 16,000 seats.

A balcony on one side holds the two-thousand-member choir and orchestra combined. On a typical Sunday evening, when the main service is held, one thousand instruments—mostly guitars, mandolins, and accordions—will be playing while all two thousand choir members are singing special numbers. While they are singing, some worshippers will begin "dancing in the Spirit" while others shout "glory to God."

But this building is inadequate because the flock numbers between eighty thousand and ninety thousand members twelve years of age and over. Members are allowed to attend the mother church only once a month. The other three Sundays they are participating in the activities of the many smaller "classes" located in the different neighborhoods of the city. The classes are like satellite churches. Their membership runs between 800 and three thousand, and each is led by one of the associate pastors. Many of the classes have their own very substantial church buildings.[3]

In the God of Love Pentecostal Church in Brazil they baptize some three thousand people every six months! This rapid growth has resulted in the acquisition of 16 radio stations across Brazil, and this in turn accelerates their growth. According to Richard Sturz of the Conservative Baptists, the total Protestant community in Brazil is now 25 million.

Paul Finkenbinder, a radio speaker in Latin America, celebrated the fortieth anniversary of his ministry in 1984. He now has a daily column in 44 newspapers and is heard one thousand times each day on 543 stations. His new television program, "A Message of Conscience," is aired daily on 12 stations.

---

3. Ibid., pp. 22, 23.

In the past, the churches in Latin America have lagged behind other regions when it comes to overseas missions, but that is changing. In May 1981, the first conference on world missions was held in Guatemala City. Some three hundred participants from 22 countries spent an entire week being exposed to what for many was a totally new concept—their responsibility for world missions.

A second conference was convened in Guatemala in July 1984. Its theme was "Latin America, Open Your Eyes." Participants included six hundred pastors, students, missionaries, and interested laymen from 17 countries. A third, and largest yet, is scheduled for 1987 in Brazil.

In May 1984, more than one thousand pastors and young people from all over Central America gathered in El Salvador for Mission '84, a conference on world missions. Mission '84 was sponsored by the young, 1,200-member Nazareth Church, located in a middle-class suburb of San Salvador. Included in Mission '84 was a seminar for pastors, designed to encourage local churches to get involved in world missions and to set up their own programs. Nazareth Church's annual mission budget is $40,000 (U.S.), which goes toward the support of missionaries in Spain, Africa, Indonesia, the Philippines, and Puerto Rico. Little wonder that El Salvador's evangelical population tripled in the last ten years, from 250,000 to 750,000.

Remote and Dangerous Places

Church growth is taking place in remote areas where missionaries are excluded. P. M. Thomas, director of the Kashmir Evangelical Fellowship, recently spoke at a convention in Kalimpong where 300 to 500 people gathered daily for five days of meetings. More than 90 percent were Nepalese. The rest were from Bhutan and Sikkim, two countries that have never been open to Western missionaries. Some 250 persons made decisions for Christ, and 47 committed themselves for missionary work. Thomas Mat-

thews, head of Rajastan Gospel Mission, recently ministered in Rangpo, Sikkim. He conducted 12 meetings in five
days, with more than 1,000 people for the evening meetings. Said he, "I saw the Holy Spirit moving among the
Sikkimese peoples. Hundreds of young people are on fire
for the Lord."

Even in the most troubled parts of the world the Holy
Spirit is working in unusual ways. In 1979 Ray McCauley
started a church in Johannesburg with 13 people. Today it
has grown to 6,000. A 16-day crusade in the capital of
Zimbabwe in 1985 resulted in 31,000 people making first-
time decisions for Christ, among them four government
officials and the wife of the prime minister, Robert
Mugabe.

In war-torn Nicaragua the churches continue to witness
and grow. One denomination, Brethren in Christ, doubled
the number of its churches from 23 to 45 in two years. In
1984 the Bible Society distributed 100,000 Bibles—more
than double the 1983 figure of 47,000.

No country has suffered more in the last ten years than
Lebanon, but even there the people, in their misery, are
responding to the gospel. One church that eight years ago
had only one congregation now has nine.

The Ways God Is at Work

Radio Work

Missionary radio is one way in which God is at work
these days. The Far East Broadcasting Company, based in
Manila, is typical of what is being done in missionary
radio today. Founded in 1945, FEBC broadcasts the gospel
over 28 transmitters for 1,900 hours each week in 101
languages of Asia, Africa, and Latin America. Broadcasting facilities are located in the Philippines, Korea, the
Seychelles in the Indian Ocean, Saipan in the Marianas,
and San Francisco. It has recording studios in Bangalore,

Beirut, Bangkok, Hong Kong, Jakarta, Manila, New Delhi, Saipan, Seoul, Singapore, and Tokyo. Cooperating studios, belonging to other mission organizations throughout Asia, supply tapes that are sent to Manila for broadcasting back to the respective countries. Millions of people hear the gospel every day by means of that one organization. FEBC broadcasts in more languages than any other organization in the world, including Radio Moscow (82) and the Voice of America (48). The response is exceptionally good. Thirty thousand letters are received every month from 60 different countries. And FEBC is only one of some 65 missionary broadcasting stations around the world!

They may not know it, but the Japanese with their high technology have made a significant contribution to world evangelization. Their tiny, cheap, dependable transistor radios are available in all parts of the Third World. There is hardly a village that doesn't have at least one transistor radio, and listening to programs is often a community affair. Radio has two great advantages: It can penetrate all the iron and bamboo curtains that were ever erected, and it can be understood by the illiterate. Pius Wakatama, one of Africa's younger leaders, has made the following statement:

> Most Africans can now afford transistor radios. Many of them are assembled in Africa and are inexpensive. All one has to do, if he lives in the village, is to sell one or two of his goats, and he will have the price of a transistor radio. He may also need to sell a chicken for the batteries. On many grass-thatched roofs today are one or two reeds joined together as antennae for transistor radios.[4]

Radio is the most important, most effective, and most economical medium for the dissemination of information on a worldwide scale. In some countries the government is

4. Pius Wakatama, *Independence for the Third World Church: An African's Perspective on Missionary Work* (Downers Grove: InterVarsity, 1976), p. 62.

placing a radio in the larger villages, hoping thereby to bring their peoples into the twentieth century. Usually these radios are in use almost around the clock; there is always somebody listening. This provides the Christian missionary with a custom-built apparatus for the world-wide proclamation of the gospel. Billy Graham speaks to more people in one broadcast than the apostle Paul was able to reach in his entire lifetime.

Nor should we overlook the tens of thousands of Christian radio programs broadcast locally in all parts of the Third World. In most instances these programs are prepared by Christian churches and aired over local stations. In some instances government-operated stations regularly give free time to Christian programs. This is the case in Kenya, Zambia, Nigeria, and other countries of Black Africa. In some countries of Latin America local radio and television stations turn the whole of Good Friday over to the Protestant churches.

In recent years churches and missions in the Third World have been getting into television. Luis Palau has had a very effective ministry in Latin America.

Each of Nigeria's 19 states has its own television station and Christian programs are being gobbled up by the producers. Some stations are on the air from noon to midnight, seven days a week. Christian programs are in great demand, and the stations not only give free time, but also pay for the programs. Because there is only one channel on each station, viewers have no choice. So popular are these broadcasts that most television sets are on almost all the time, with about ten people in front of each set. The television mania is such that even Muslims will watch Christian programs. One Muslim chief refuses to receive visitors while the "Christian Half Hour" is on!

Bible Correspondence Courses

Bible correspondence courses have played a major role in the Third World. The first course goes back many years and continues strong today. Bible correspondence courses are very popular in the Muslim world, where freedom of religion does not exist. Muslims who would not dare attend a Christian church are willing to study the Scriptures in the solitude and security of their own homes. The Gospel Missionary Union began work in Morocco in 1894, but after 90 years of arduous and dangerous work, there is not one organized indigenous church in the country. In 1960 GMU tried something new. An ad in the local newspapers invited Muslims to study Christianity by means of a Bible correspondence course. Only a post-office box number was furnished. To the surprise of almost everyone, some 18,000 persons signed up to study the Gospel of John. A few years later the North Africa Mission used the same plan in Tunisia and 20,000 responded.

Operation Mobilization had a similar experience in Iran. In Bangladesh, between 1960 and 1980, more than 50,000 persons enrolled in Bible correspondence courses offered by the International Christian Fellowship. Half were Muslims and half were Hindus. The Light of Life correspondence course started by Don Hillis in India and the many Emmaus Bible courses sponsored by the Brethren have been used with great effect in all parts of the world. Radio stations, such as HCJB in Quito and FEBC in Manila, conduct Bible institutes of the air and hundreds of thousands of listeners have enrolled in their courses.

Religion in Public Schools

Another unique opportunity for the dissemination of the gospel is the teaching of a course known as Religious Knowledge in the public schools of Africa. In the "good old days" if the missionaries wished to teach the Bible to the children of Africa they had to build and maintain schools. Now they are invited to teach Christianity in the tax-supported schools without any administrative responsibilities or financial obligations. They are not responsible for attendance, discipline, or anything else, and they are actually paid to do the job. The course is required in the high schools of such former British colonies as Ghana, Nigeria, Kenya, Uganda, and Tanzania. The textbook is the Bible. The final exams are set by the Department of Education, and the students must pass if they wish to graduate. The teacher, frequently a missionary, is free to conduct the class in any way he or she wishes, provided the material is adequately covered.

Similar opportunities exist elsewhere in the world. In Indonesia one missionary was recently hired by the government to prepare a complete curriculum for the teaching of Religious Knowledge (in this case, Christianity) in the entire school system of Indonesia. We never had that kind of opportunity in the "good old days."

Bible Translation and Distribution

In the area of Bible translation we see the same momentum. Perhaps the greatest contribution made by the missionaries has been the translation of the Bible. Today the Scriptures are available in 1,829 languages and dialects of the world. The complete Bible is available to 90 percent of the world's population in the vernacular (in 293 languages). The complete New Testament is available to another 5 percent (in 618 languages). And at least one book, usually called a Portion, is available to another 3 percent (in 918 languages). This leaves only 2 percent of the world's population without any part of the Holy Scriptures.

Whenever Bible translation is mentioned we naturally think of first-time translations, and these, of course, are very important; but they are not the whole story. Languages change, and sooner or later new translations become necessary. This is called revision rather than translation. At present the United Bible Societies (comprising 100 independent national societies) is working with some three thousand missionary-linguists at work on eight hundred different projects, most of them revisions of earlier translations.

Unique among all the faith missions is Wycliffe Bible Translators. Since its beginning in 1935 its translators have worked in more than one thousand languages and dialects. To date Wycliffe has produced more than two hundred complete New Testaments and a new one is coming off the press every 15 days. With 5,500 workers on its roll, WBT is concentrating on the 200,000,000 people, speaking more than three thousand dialects, who are still waiting for their first book of the Bible. To achieve this, they are forging ahead with all possible speed, beginning work in a new dialect every 21 days.

Equally exciting is the worldwide distribution of the Scriptures. In 1984, the United Bible Societies reported a total distribution of more than 500,000,000 copies of the Scriptures in well over a thousand languages. No other book in the world has ever been so widely distributed. And in spite of unsettled conditions in many parts of the world, the rate of distribution continues to rise steadily year after year.

According to a recent report, the annual increase in distribution in the Middle East was 82 percent, in Mexico, 117 percent, in Iran 155 percent, and in Czechoslovakia 522 percent. Even in China Bibles are being published and distributed by the China Christian Council.

In Angola, most people are lucky to get one square meal a day; yet when a shipment of two thousand Bibles recently reached the capital, Luanda, Angolans lined up for hours to get a copy. They waited patiently in line through the following day until the supplies ran out.

About the same time a shipment of Bibles arrived in Mozambique. There, the Bibles were snapped up not only by the local people but also by visitors from Eastern Europe. In a half-hour period, Russians were seen leaving the Bible society with 20 Bibles in their possession! John Dean of the United Bible Societies, who was on hand to witness the scene, said, "There is hunger not only for food, but a spiritual hunger in both countries for the Word of God."[5]

Missions Based in the Third World

One of the most exciting developments in the area of Christian missions is the recent upsurge in missionary interest and support on the part of the churches in the Third World. Too long we have subscribed to the notion that the evangelization of the world is the "white man's burden." That may have been true in the nineteenth century. Certainly it is no longer true in the latter part of the twentieth century.

In recent years, particularly in the last two decades, there has been an enormous increase in the number of missionaries sent out and supported by Third World organizations. A study in 1972 indicated that there were slightly more than 3,000 such missionaries serving with some 203 agencies. Eight years later the number had increased to 15,250 missionaries under 368 agencies. Today the figure is closer to 18,000. According to Lawrence E. Keyes, "Non-Western missionary recruitment for full-time cross-cultural endeavor appears to be growing at least five times as fast as recruitment for missions in North America."[6]

The four countries with the largest number of missionaries are Nigeria (2,500), India (4,200), Ghana (1,127), and Kenya (1,002). National churches with the largest number of missionaries are the Church of the Lord "Aladura" in Nigeria (1,250), the Burmese Baptist Convention (887), the Evangelical Lutheran Church of Papua New Guinea (450), the Evangelical Missionary Society of Nigeria (440), and the Brazilian Baptist Convention (370). Not many churches in the West can match the record of these churches!

In many countries, especially in Asia, evangelical missionary agencies are forming nationwide associations.

5. *Missionary News Service,* February 1, 1984, p. 3.
6. *Missionary News Service,* July 1, 1982.

Japan, India, the Philippines, Thailand, Korea, and Malaysia all have such associations. Financial support, which used to be such a problem, is stronger than ever. In 1985 the Yoido Full Gospel Church in Seoul was supporting 143 missionaries to the tune of $12 million a year in United States currency. The overseas national churches of the Seventh-day Adventists are now giving more than $20 million a year to foreign missions around the world.

Some 40 mission leaders from all six continents gathered in Bangalore in January 1982 to discuss two major themes: training missionaries and partnership between Western and non-Western missions. To this end, missionary training schools are being established in various places around the world. In 1976 the Indian Missionary Training Institute was launched as a partnership between the India Evangelical Mission and BMMF International. Since then other missions have been using this institute. Just recently the Union Biblical Seminary in Pune, India, has established a department of missions. Seminaries in Korea are doing the same.

In 1984 missiologists from Africa, Asia, and Latin America gathered in Mexico to discuss the work of the Holy Spirit in missions. The conference was called by Samuel Escobar of Peru, David Gitari of Kenya, and Vinay Samuel of India. This was the second such conference on this   theme; the first was held in Bangkok in 1982.

In 1985, 140 evangelists from 14 Asian countries gathered in Singapore to dicuss how best to reach Asia's 2.5 billion people with the gospel. The conference was sponsored by the Asia Evangelical Fellowship as part of its twenty-fifth anniversary celebration. Topics discussed in the workshop included literature, music, slum-dwellers, prisoners, children, those of other faiths, and tourists.

International Students in the United States

International students in this country are showing an unprecedented interest in world missions. In 1985 some

150 African Christians from 15 countries convened a conference in Columbus, Texas, the purpose of which was to develop mission awareness among the African students. The conference was sponsored by the African Christian Students Fellowship, which has five hundred members on 35 campuses.

For years the churches in Europe have lacked evangelistic zeal and missionary passion, but that too is changing. The more than 2,500 students who have graduated from Greater Europe Mission's ten Bible colleges are beginning to make their presence felt. During the Christmas break in 1982 the European Missionary Association sponsored a missions rally, known as Mission '83, attended by seven thousand participants from 42 countries. More than 250 Christian organizations were represented in the exhibition hall. Mission '83 was specifically designed to promote missionary vision and involvement among European youth.

The Future Advance of Missions

Not content with the achievements of the past, many churches and organizations are gearing up for further advance in the future. Campus Crusade for Christ, with 12,000 full-time and part-time staff in 150 countries, expects to show the "Jesus" film to two to three billion people in the next decade. This film has already been translated into more than two hundred languages. Follow-up plans for those who make decisions include tapes of 90 sermons, along with literature that will be left in every village. Beginning in December 1985, CCC plans to train 100,000 students to reach the world for Christ through a worldwide satellite hookup. Bill Bright wants to reach every campus in the world by 1990.

The OMS International in 1981 set a new ten-year goal of one million conversions, half a million church members and two thousand new churches in 14 countries. Both

Sudan Interior Mission and Overseas Crusades plan to double their staff by 1990.

In 1984 the Presbyterian Church in America adopted a ten-year plan to double its missionary force from four hundred to eight hundred. This is, indeed, welcome news, when so many of the mainline denominations over the last 20 years have been reducing their commitment to world missions.

The Role of the Chinese

No ethnic group is in a better position to evangelize the world than the Chinese. In 1976 they held a Congress on World Evangelization in Hong Kong, which attracted 1,600 Chinese leaders from all over the world. A second congress, convened in Singapore in 1981, was attended by 1,200 leaders. At that congress they drew up a 30-year plan—divided into three decades—for the multiplication of Chinese churches around the world. A third congress is planned for August 1986 in Taiwan.

The Chinese are now the largest group of Orientals in North America. Large colonies of them are found in San Francisco, New York, Vancouver, and Toronto. Altogether there are more than six hundred Chinese churches in the United States and Canada, and they are growing in strength and numbers every year. In recent years their missionary vision has been kindled to the point where they are now holding annual missionary conferences, promoting the idea of the faith promise, and in other ways advancing the cause of missions around the world.

The first Chinese missionary convention in Canada was held in August 1985 at Guelph University in Ontario. Reported as an "exciting event," the convention attracted one thousand participants, among them 140 pastors and other full-time Christian workers. More than a dozen Chinese missionaries were on hand and participated in the various workshops.

To date there are not many full-time Chinese Christian workers, largely because of parental pressure; but if the day ever comes when this impasse is broken, we may find many Chinese volunteering for missionary service.

If the rapidly growing church in China ever regains full religious freedom and is permitted to send and support missionaries overseas, China, in the twenty-first century, may provide the lion's share of Christian missionaries. Their Asian background, their ability to adapt to other cultures and learn other languages, their ability to endure hardship ("eat bitterness," as they call it), and their reputation for integrity, frugality, and hard work will stand them in good stead when they go out to win the world for Christ.

For those interested in additional information about Third World missions, several books are available: *The How and Why of Third World Missions* and *Readings in Third World Missions* by Marlin L. Nelson and *The Last Age of Missions* by Lawrence E. Keyes. All three may be obtained from the William Carey Library, P. O. Box 40129, Pasadena, California 91104.

2

What Kind of World Is It?

The world for which Christ died is a rapidly changing, highly complex, and tragically confused world. The world has always had its share of problems but the problems of this postwar period surpass anything we have known before. There is hardly a major area of the world that isn't facing unprecedented problems that appear to defy human solution.

A Divided World

The United Nations was founded in 1945 on the assumption that the wartime cooperation between the United States and the Soviet Union would carry over into the postwar period. Alas, it turned out to be a gratuitous assumption. Imagine the peace and prosperity that might have accrued if the two superpowers had been able to cooperate instead of compete! Politically, the world is divided into three parts. The First World includes the United States and its allies. The Soviet Union and its allies form the Second World. The remaining nations are usually lumped together as the Third World. The phrase was first used at the Bandung Conference in 1955, and has been used ever since.

Industrially, the world is divided between the developed

nations and the undeveloped nations, which prefer to be called developing nations. The developed nations have an extensive industrial base to their economies; hence their standard of living is higher. The others—mostly in the Third World—have an agricultural base to their economies; consequently their standard of living tends to be lower, in some cases much lower.

Economically, the world is divided between the rich nations and the poor nations. In spite of all the foreign-aid programs on the part of the rich countries, the gap between the two parts of the world is increasing year after year; so much so that some people believe that unless something different—something drastic—is done, the "revolution of rising expectations" will one day lead to an explosion of serious proportions. The illegal immigration of aliens, mostly Mexicans, into the United States may well portend a coming catastrophe of horrendous proportions.

Those of us who have the good fortune to live in the United States have little understanding of the deep-seated problems of the Third World. We have lived with our affluence so long that we have come to take it for granted. Some of the smaller countries could live on the food that we throw into the trash can. To make matters worse, our efforts to help have been largely ineffective; and in the process we have made as many enemies as friends.

A Physically Diseased World

Life expectancy in much of the world is between 40 and 60 years, depending on the country. In some countries half of the children die before the age of seven, and in many cases the parents don't have the satisfaction of knowing what caused the death. Tuberculosis is common, even in such an advanced country as Taiwan. Leprosy is a major problem in Thailand. Dysentery, caused by contaminated food and water, is a big killer of children.

Malnutrition, of course, is endemic. It is estimated that half the world's population goes to bed hungry every night. Malnutrition is particularly hard on children. It affects not only the body, but the brain as well; and once the brain has been impaired the damage is irrevocable. In the West "famine" is a word to be found only in the dictionary. In many parts of the world, drought is a perennial problem and famine is never far away. One poor harvest and the peasants face starvation. The hunger problem has been compounded by the large number of refugees—millions of them—who are the victims of war.

The World Health Organization has made significant gains in the war against malaria, smallpox, and other diseases; but in spite of its gargantuan efforts tens of millions of people are without the rudiments of a health delivery system. It must be said to the credit of Communist China that the government has done an unusually effective job in this area. Tens of thousands of "barefoot" doctors and community nurses are making modern medicine available to nearly every town and village in rural China. When one remembers that there are more than one billion people in China, this is no mean achievement. Alas, the record in many other parts of the world is not nearly as good.

It is difficult for us to realize that in many parts of the Third World much of what we take for granted is entirely missing. Imagine a country where the people have no knowledge of germs, where personal hygiene is unknown, and where public sanitation is nonexistent. For centuries they have been eating contaminated food and drinking impure water without knowing it. When half the children die, they blame it on evil spirits. And when missionaries and others have tried to alleviate the situation, their efforts have not always been appreciated. Dr. Tom Hale, writing in regard to a small town in Nepal, has this to say:

> You would think that a town so burdened with sickness and suffering of all kinds that has never seen a doctor or

nurse until recent years would cry out for medical help and welcome us with open arms and tears of gratitude. . . . In their eyes we've merely come to take their money in exchange for some trifling medicine of untested worth and very likely with an ulterior motive besides.

Hale goes on to describe the unsanitary conditions in the same town:

To set foot in the town is to step back a thousand years. In distinction to the capital, where at least the sewage flows along open gutters along each street, here there are no gutters. In a more jaundiced moment, the entire town could be likened to one great toilet for goats, pigs, chickens, cows and humans; and your nose would not belie it.[1]

On a more personal level, imagine people enduring headaches, earaches, and toothaches without even an aspirin to relieve the pain. Imagine a family that has never seen a toothbrush, a cake of soap, or a roll of toilet paper. Sickness, weakness, pain, and premature death are simply a way of life in many parts of the world.

A Poverty-stricken World

The outstanding characteristic of the Third World is poverty. It is the thing that rises up and smites the Western tourist in the face. It, more than anything else, accounts for the backwardness of these countries. Ignorance, illiteracy, disease, malnutrition, and many other problems all stem from poverty, and could be eliminated in record time if the economic level of the people could be substantially raised.

Just how poor is the Third World? It is so poor that it has recently been divided into two parts—and one part is now referred to as the Fourth World. It includes 45 countries

---

1. *Prayer Letter,* March 21, 1974.

with less than $300 in annual output per person. At a World Hunger Conference, convened in Rome by the United Nations, some countries were regarded as so hopeless, from an economic point of view, that they were referred to as "basket cases." This reflected a judgment that, regardless of how much help they might receive, the people in the long run could not be saved from starvation.

The poverty of the Fourth World must be seen to be believed. We have poverty here in the United States, but it is a mild form of affluence compared with the poverty elsewhere. Our ghettos are gardens compared with the shantytowns that have grown up around Calcutta, Lima, Mexico City, Nairobi, Cairo, and other metropolitan centers. The poverty level for a family of four in the United States is close to $10,000 a year! With that kind of income people in the Fourth World would regard themselves as millionaires.

In spite of all the foreign-aid programs emanating from the West, the situation in many parts of the world has deteriorated in the past 25 years. This is especially true of the continent of Africa with almost 500 million people. Independence was expected to usher in an era of unprecedented prosperity. With the imperialists out of the way, the nationals would be able to reap the rewards of their own hard labor. Unfortunately, this did not happen. The dreams that came with nationhood have long since disappeared. Today the picture is bleak indeed. Famine, inflation, unemployment, and a high population growth rate plague most of the former colonies. Even Nigeria, Africa's most populous country, once swimming in oil revenues, has recently sent two million imported workers back to Ghana, Cameroon, and other countries.

In some areas, such as Ethiopia, Uganda, and the Sahel, untold misery has been caused by prolonged drought. In other places it has been the result of poor planning, mismanagement, and widespread corruption. President Mobutu of Zaire, with a personal fortune estimated at four billion dollars, is reputed to be the richest man in Africa;

whereas the average worker in the capital earns only one-tenth of what he earned in 1960 when Zaire received its independence.

Some of the misery is due to the civil wars—really tribal wars—that devastated Nigeria, Chad, Sudan, Burundi, Uganda, and other countries. The foreign minister of Togo says flatly: "Africa is dying." An official of the Organization for African Unity is more specific. He says, "If things continue as they are only eight or nine countries of the present 50 will survive the next few years."[2]

Added to the domestic problems of these nations has been the spiraling cost of oil that has taxed their financial resources to the breaking point. In order to remain solvent, the African nations have borrowed heavily from the World Bank, the International Monetary Fund, and Western commercial banks. The total foreign debt owed by Third World nations now stands at $800 billion, and Western bankers worry they will declare bankruptcy and destroy the entire fabric of world finance. Ghana, Kenya, Malawi, Zaire, and Tanzania are spending ten times as much for oil as they did in 1973, when the oil crisis began. Other countries, once self-sufficient in staples, are now having to spend their hard-earned foreign currency on food. One-third of the African countries are now reporting areas of starvation. In East Africa alone an estimated 60 million people face the prospect of prolonged hunger.

It would not be so bad if the future held any promise, but such is not the case. G. E. A. Lardner, an economist in Sierra Leone, says, "On the basis of all the economic projections we have seen so far, Africa in the year 2000 will not be in the ditch it is in now—it will be in the bottom of a deep, black hole."[3]

The situation in Latin America is not much better. Mexico squandered its oil revenue in the 1970s and today has a foreign debt of $96 billion and an unemployment rate of 40 percent. Most of the estimated seven million illegal immi-

---

2. *U.S. News and World Report,* July 28, 1980, p. 47.
3. Ibid.

grants now in the United States came from Mexico, and there is no relief in sight. The root cause of the civil wars now threatening to engulf Central America is economic rather than political. The masses are desperate and see no peaceful way out of the economic morass. They will welcome and support anyone—including the Communists—who will promise help.

There are some bright spots in Asia. Japan leads the way, with South Korea, Taiwan, Hong Kong, and Singapore not far behind. Most of the other countries lag far behind. The three large countries of India, Pakistan, and Bangladesh are among the poorest countries in the world. In fact, they belong to the Fourth World. The gains achieved by a succession of Five-Year Plans in India have been wiped out by a steady increase in population. It is difficult to see how a country as large as India, with 750 million people, can ever significantly raise its overall standard of living without a major economic and industrial breakthrough. There are just too many mouths to fill.

Conditions in Pakistan and Bangladesh are even worse. Almost without exception the peasants, who form 80 percent of the population, are desperately poor and exist on 1,500 calories a day. To some extent the poverty in the Third World is perpetuated by the unscrupulous policies of the powerful multinational corporations based in the West. Such is the economic and industrial power of the United States that other countries, directly or indirectly, are affected by what happens here. The *New York Times,* on August 30, 1983, stated, "Each time mortgage rates in the United States rise one percentage point, 1500 forest workers in British Columbia are laid off." One-crop economies in Latin America are very vulnerable to the vagaries of international trade. When import tariffs are raised one or two points, thousands of people are out of work.

A Socially Deprived World

It is difficult, if not impossible, for the average American to appreciate the extent to which the people of the

Third World lack the simplest things that are a regular part of the American way of life: daily newspapers, weekly magazines, television programs, shopping malls, super-markets, postal service, public utilities, four-lane high-ways, high-school and college bands, professional sports, public libraries, churches, parks, playgrounds, swimming pools, McDonald's, Baskin Robbins, Sears Roebuck, Greyhound buses, 40-hour work weeks, summer vaca-tions, sick leave, medical, life, and other forms of insur-ance.

Transportation of the rapid, safe, and convenient kind found in the United States is virtually unknown in the rural areas of the Third World. All-weather roads are rare. Dirt roads turn into quagmires after half an hour of rain. Peasants walk to market, hauling their produce with them. The donkey, the ox cart, and the wheelbarrow are still the main modes of transportation. In the towns and smaller cities, people depend on bicycles, pedicabs, and other manpowered vehicles. The "wealthy" cab drivers have jeepneys built for six or eight, often with twice that number crowded in.

Imagine a village without a school, or a school without a library. Imagine children without toys or students with-out books. It all seems so unreal to us, but for people in the developing countries it is a way of life. Ask any Peace Corps volunteer and he or she will tell you what it is like to teach school in Nepal, Niger, Afghanistan, the Philip-pines, or any other of the 90 countries in which the Peace Corps has worked.

In much of the Third World women and girls are second-class citizens. They are virtually beasts of burden, gather-ing fuel, carrying water, cooking meals, and making clothes. They eat only after the menfolk have been fed. In the Orient parents still prefer boys to girls. Only in recent times have girls been given an education; in every case female education was introduced by the missionaries, often over the protests of the parents. One Hindu father, when asked to send his daughter to the mission school,

replied, "You mean you want to educate my *daughter*?
Next you'll want to educate my cow."

Governments in the Third World are doing their best to
enforce compulsory education at the elementary level, and
commendable progress has been made. But the problem of
illiteracy has not yet been solved. While the rate of illiteracy is dropping each year, the *number* of illiterates in the
world continues to increase, and today stands at 800 million.

Reasons for this are many. To begin with, there are not
enough schools to meet the need. In addition, truancy is an
ongoing problem, especially during harvest time. The
drop-out rate is very high. Peasants need their children in
the fields, so they take them out of school.

At the secondary level, there is an even greater shortage
of schools than at the primary level. For this reason only a
small fraction of grade-school graduates are able to go on
to high school. At the college level, the competition for
admission is fierce, with only about 5 percent of high-
school graduates entering college. Someone has said that
a wasted mind is a terrible thing. Alas, there are hundreds
of millions of wasted minds in the world.

The deprivation common in the Third World naturally
spills over into the churches. Christian centers on the mission field fall into three categories: preaching points,
small congregations, and organized churches. Needless to
say, the first two do not have adequately trained laymen,
much less pastors. And very few of such leaders as there
are have had any formal theological training. In Brazil,
for example, only 3,000 of the 59,600 pastors in the Assemblies of God have had even Bible-school training. Indeed,
many of them are either illiterate or only semiliterate.
The only books they possess are a Bible and a hymnbook.

Of the full-time pastors, only a small number are ordained, and these are usually overworked and underpaid.
Ordained pastors in the Church of South India have the
oversight of anywhere from 10 to 20 congregations. The
great Batak Church of Indonesia, with two million mem-

bers, has only two hundred ordained pastors. And even the ordained men are not all seminary graduates. Many have not gone beyond Bible school. Very few of them have the literary tools we in the United States take for granted. In many places Sunday-school and Christian-education materials are unknown. Even a one-volume Bible dictionary may not be available.

Many of the churches, through no fault of their own, are poorly organized and inadequately equipped, at least by Western standards. Not one pastor in a hundred enjoys the luxury of a study or a library in either home or church. As for separate buildings for Sunday school, they are unheard of. In some places the Christians meet in the open air. If they have a building, it is usually an ordinary house with one or two partitions removed to provide additional space. There is no ceiling; only a thatched roof which often leaks when it rains. Windows, if they exist at all, are merely openings in the wall. If seats are available they are usually backless benches—"sawhorses," we call them. If not, the church members squat on the earthern floor.

A Politically Unsettled World

One does not have to be a student of political science to know that the world is seething with unrest. Riot and revolution are the order of the day. We hoped that the United Nations, founded with such high hopes in San Francisco in 1945, would be able to maintain peace throughout the world. Alas, the United Nations has been only partially successful. Doubtless it would have been more successful had the Soviet Union used the veto in the Security Council less frequently.

In some parts of the world governments rise and fall almost with the barometer. Traffic moves back and forth between prison and parliament, and the jails are filled with political prisoners of one stripe or another. In Africa there were 11 wars and at least 51 coups between 1956—

the beginning of independence—and 1980. Countries that have not experienced a coup, successful or abortive, can be numbered on the fingers of one hand.

The situation in Asia has not been any better. Civil wars have occurred in Malaysia, the Philippines, Pakistan, Indonesia, Burma, Laos, Cambodia, and Vietnam. India and Pakistan have gone to war three times over Kashmir. West Pakistan launched a war against East Pakistan and in the process created ten million refugees who fled across the border into India.

In the People's Republic of China, millions were liquidated as "enemies of the people" in the early 1950s and tens of thousands were killed during the Great Proletarian Cultural Revolution (1966–69). In Cambodia the Pol Pot regime committed genocide on its own people by killing an estimated two million persons. Martial law has been declared in Korea, the Philippines, and other countries. Even in India, one of the few genuine democracies in Asia, Indira Gandhi was obliged to declare a 19-month state of emergency in the 1970s. Following the assassination of Mrs. Gandhi in October 1984 by two Sikh bodyguards, several thousand innocent Sikhs were slaughtered in various parts of India.

In the Middle East peace has been achieved between Israel and Egypt, but the other Arab nations adamantly refuse to make a deal with Israel. War continues between Iran and Iraq, and if Iran wins there is fear that the fanatical Muslim revolution will spill over into the Gulf States. For the last ten years Lebanon has been tortured by an on-again-off-again war that defies solution.

In Latin America the pattern is much the same—riots, revolutions, palace coups, wars, guerrilla activity, death squads, and other forms of violence. The hot spot at the moment is Central America where Cuba and the Soviet Union are aiding and abetting wars of liberation in Nicaragua, El Salvador, Honduras, and Guatemala. The invasion of Grenada by the United States in 1983 may have given pause, at least for the time being, to Cuban and

Soviet ambitions in Central America, but peace based on justice is still only a future hope.

Even in the Communist countries of Eastern Europe there have been periods of unrest—East Germany in 1953, Hungary in 1956, Czechoslovakia in 1968, and Poland, 1980–83. Only the massive military might of the Soviet Union has kept those regimes in power so long. In September 1983 the world was shocked when the Soviet Union shot down an unarmed Korean plane with 269 persons on board—all of whom died in the crash.

And so it goes, on and on, and around the world. Science and technology have enabled man to control almost everything—everything except himself. Surely Isaiah was right when he said:

> The wicked are like the tossing sea,
> For it cannot be quiet,
> And its waters toss up refuse and mud.
> [Is 57:20]

It goes without saying that both the Christian mission and the Christian church are affected by conditions such as these. In Burundi a whole generation of pastors was wiped out in tribal warfare in the 1960s. In Colombia scores of national pastors were killed during La Violencia from 1948 to 1960. In Cambodia the fledgling church was destroyed following the American withdrawal from South Vietnam in 1975. The archbishop of the Anglican Church in Uganda was murdered in cold blood by the agents of Idi Amin. Other bishops barely escaped with their lives. In several countries in Latin America the Wycliffe Bible Translators have been accused of being agents of the Central Intelligence Agency and threatened with expulsion. In Zaire, in 1964, some 200 missionaries, most of them Roman Catholics, were hacked to pieces by the Simbas and thrown to the crocodiles. In the 1970s 39 missionaries and their children were killed by the antigovernment guerrillas in Rhodesia, now Zimbabwe. In Thailand the Overseas Missionary Fellowship lost 5 missionaries, 2 of whom were held several months for ransom that was never paid. In Colombia Chet Bitterman met with the same fate.

It has been said, doubtless with some truth, that there have been more Christian martyrs in the twentieth century than in any previous century. And the future may well be more difficult and dangerous than the past. If so, we may have to call for Christian commandos who will agree to remain single for at least one full term of service in order to get the job done. Some parts of the world are just too dangerous for women and children.

A Spiritually Lost World

To fully appreciate the lostness of man we must go back to the time of his innocence in the Garden of Eden. The Bible clearly teaches that man in the beginning was made not only *by* God but *for* God, and that God intended man to find his highest happiness not in his possessions or his achievements but in fellowship with Himself.

But man did not retain his innocence very long. Knowing full well the prohibition placed upon him by God, man deliberately partook of the forbidden fruit. Instantly something happened—sin came into his life and God went out. From that day to this man has wandered to and fro on the face of the earth as a spiritual vagabond. He has sailed the seven seas; he has traveled to the ends of the earth; he has even visited the moon. He has founded empires and dynasties; he has built cities and castles; he has heaped to himself riches and honor; but for all that his *soul* is an orphan still. There is in his heart a God-shaped blank that nothing on earth can ever fill. His spirit, like Noah's dove, flits back and forth between "rough seas and stormy skies." He is unable to find what Jesus called "rest for the soul." With the vertical connection broken, all horizontal connections are at loose ends. In a sentence: *He is lost.*

The question is often asked: What about the heathen who have never heard the gospel? Are they lost? And we

must answer: Yes, they are lost. *All* men are lost. That goes
for the "pagans" in America just as much as the "heathen"
in Africa. However, when dealing with the so-called heathen—devotees of the non-Christian religions—certain
truths must be kept in mind.

1. *The heathen were not "heathen" to begin with.* They
became heathen when they deliberately gave up the
knowledge of God. In the first chapter of Romans Paul
describes the moral and spiritual declension of the human
race. He says, "For although they knew God they did not
honor him as God or give thanks to him, but they *became*
futile in their thinking and their senseless minds were
darkened. Claiming to be wise, they *became* fools, and
exchanged the glory of the immortal God for images re-
sembling mortal man or birds or animals or reptiles"
(Rom 1:21–23, rsv, italics added).

2. *In their progressive apostasy the heathen did not lose*
all *knowledge of God.* They retained a knowledge of His
eternal power and deity which reached them through
creation. "For what can be known about God is plain to
them, because God has shown it to them. Ever since the
creation of the world his invisible nature, namely, his eternal power and deity, has been clearly perceived in the
things that have been made" (Rom 1:19–20, rsv).

3. *The revelation of God through creation is supple-*
mented by another revelation that comes through nature or
providence. Speaking to the animists of Lycaonia, Paul
said, "He [God] did not leave Himself without witness, in
that He did good and gave you rains from heaven and
fruitful seasons, satisfying your hearts with food and glad-
ness" (Acts 14:17). Nearly every heathen society has some
knowledge, however vague, of a great Spirit in the sky who
has the power of life and death, who causes the sun to shine
and the rain to fall. Consequently they have religious ritu-
als by which they celebrate a good harvest. Alas, the thank
offerings on such occasions are offered to the earth god or
the rain god, not to the Creator of heaven and earth. But

the recognition is there. God has not left Himself without witness, as Paul said.

4. *There is still another form of light—the light of conscience.* The heathen have neither the light of the law nor the light of the gospel, but they do have the light of conscience. Paul says, "When Gentiles who do not have the Law do instinctively the things of the Law, these, not having the Law, are a law to themselves, in that they show the work of the Law written in their hearts, their conscience bearing witness, and their thoughts alternately accusing or else defending them" (Rom 2:14–15). Conscience is by no means a perfect instrument, and it can be abused to the point where it fails to function properly; but it still remains the divine monitor within the human breast. No person is so low in the moral scale that his conscience ceases to function.

We must conclude then that all have sinned and come short of the glory of God (Rom 3:23); that all men are living and dying in spiritual darkness (2 Cor 4:4); and unless they repent their eternal destiny will be everlasting destruction (2 Th 1:9).

Once man closed his eyes to the light of divine revelation he shut himself up to moral and spiritual blindness. And he has been in this state of darkness so long that he has actually come to terms with it. Jesus said, "Men loved the darkness rather than the light; for their deeds were evil" (Jn 3:19). It is a fearful indictment of the human race; but it is a fact that man has lived in darkness so long that he has come to love it. In other words, he has become naturalized in the unnatural. The mind that was made for light now delights in darkness (Eph 4:17–18). The heart that was made for love is now filled with hate (Tit 3:3). The will that was made for freedom is now enslaved to sin (Rom 7:19–21). It is not a pretty picture, but it is entirely realistic. We have it on the authority of Jesus Himself that the world is lost and unless men repent they will all perish (Jn 3:16).

And what is said about the heathen in other parts of the

world is equally true of people living in the so-called Christian world. Indeed, Americans who have lived all their lives within the sound of a church bell will have a harder time in the day of judgment than will the benighted peoples in the non-Christian part of the world.

All have sinned and come short of the glory of God, says the apostle Paul (Rom 3:23). And the *whole* world lies in the power of the evil one, says the apostle John (1 Jn 5:19).

3

Whose World: God's, Man's, or Satan's?

As far as we know ours is the only planet in the solar system that has life on it. This in itself makes our earth unique. The fact that we have placed men on the moon doesn't alter the uniqueness of this planet. We are talking about populating some of the other planets, beginning with the moon; but I doubt very much that this will ever be economically or ecologically viable. This "late, great planet earth" is our home and we do well to understand its origin, ownership, and destiny.

In the biblical worldview three persons have been involved in the unfolding of world history, God, man, and Satan. We shall consider them in reverse order.

Satan, the Invader, Usurper, and Spoiler

Satan was not always the monster of iniquity that he is today. When first created, he was "full of wisdom and perfect in beauty" (Ez 28:12). He was in fact the highest archangel in heaven. Not being content with this lofty status, he decided to challenge the authority of God. His declaration of defiance was expressed in five *I wills:*

"I will ascend to heaven;

I will raise my throne above the stars of God,
And I will sit on the mount of assembly
In the recesses of the north.
I will ascend above the heights of the clouds;
I will make myself like the Most High." [Is 14:13–14]

This was outright treason, something God could not tolerate. As a result Satan was cast out of heaven. Unable to
usurp God's authority in heaven, Satan decided to destroy
God's handiwork on earth. This he did in the Garden of
Eden when he persuaded Adam and Eve to join him in his
rebellion against God. From that time to the present this
earth has been the scene of his greatest activity and
achievement.

It was God's original intention that man should be fruitful and multiply and replenish the earth. In this way His
dominion would gradually extend over the whole earth.
Instead, because of the Fall, it was the kingdom of Satan
that was extended throughout the world, for when we
come to the New Testament we read that "the whole world
lies in the power of the evil one" (1 Jn 5:19). Moreover,
Satan is described as the "god of this world" (2 Cor 4:4), in
which capacity he demands man's worship. He is also
called the "prince of the power of the air" (Eph 2:2), and as
such he demands man's service.

It is obvious then that Satan is here in full force; but it
should be understood that the world does not really belong
to him. He is an outsider, an invader, a usurper, and a
spoiler. The power structure that he has established in the
world has no legitimacy in the divine order. His government is an alien government and all his emissaries are
quislings. As long as Satan remains in power, this planet is
occupied territory. Let us make no mistake about it. Satan
is mankind's enemy number one. He is the great spoiler.
No one understood this better than Martin Luther, who
wrote:

> For still our ancient foe
> Doth seek to work us woe;
> His craft and power are great,
> And armed with cruel hate,
> On earth is not his equal.

When General Douglas MacArthur, after losing the Battle of Bataan, left the Philippines and transferred his headquarters to Australia in 1942, he made a broadcast to the Filipino people that ended with the famous words: "I shall return!" During his absence, the Japanese army overran the archipelago, imposing its iron will on the hapless victims of its ruthless aggression. Two years later, MacArthur, true to his word, waded ashore with the first wave of American soldiers to land on the island of Leyte. In a matter of hours the good news spread fast and far: "MacArthur has returned!" War widows wept for joy. Strong men trembled with emotion. College students gathered in little groups to discuss the momentous news. MacArthur was on his way!

In a similar way, only on a grander scale, Satan invaded this planet in the dawn of human history, and for four thousand years held mankind in bondage. As the archenemy of God and man he marched to and fro throughout the earth "working his woe." Men and nations bowed before him. Kings and princes trembled at his word. Thrones and kingdoms rose and fell at his behest (Is 14:16–17). From the beggar on the dunghill to the king on his throne, all men everywhere jumped at the crack of his whip. In the words of Jesus, the strong man kept his house, and his goods were safe (Mt 12:22–29).

Then one day, at the height of his power, something happened. A Warrior from another world, the Captain of our salvation, made a landing at a place called Bethlehem and established a beachhead. Immediately the fight was joined. Satan fought with all the fury at his command. King Herod, the tool of the evil one, struck the first blow when he ordered the destruction of all male children under two years of age. The movement went underground and didn't emerge until 30 years later in the wilderness of Judea. There, for the very first time, Satan came face to face with a Man who was his equal—nay, his superior. Three times, with consummate skill, he hurled his fiery darts. One by one they fell to the ground, shattered in a thousand pieces.

That was but the first of many encounters, but it was proof and promise of victory all along the line. The holy war was by no means over, but the first decisive battle marked the turning of the tide.

One stated purpose of the Incarnation was to "destroy the works of the devil" (1 Jn 3:8). Disease, death, and demons are all part of the kingdom of Satan that Jesus came to destroy; that is why He "went about doing good, and healing all who were oppressed by the devil" (Acts 10:38). The conflict of the ages reached its climax at the cross. It was there that Christ administered the fatal blow to the enemy. It was through death that He destroyed him who had the power of death, that is, the devil; by so doing He delivered all those who through fear of death were subject to bondage (Heb 2:14–15).

Paul tells us that it was on the cross that Christ "disarmed the principalities and powers and made a public example of them, triumphing over them in [it]" (Col 2:15, RSV). Charles John Ellicott, in his *Commentary,* has this to say: "Taking his metaphor from a Roman triumph, St. Paul represents Him as passing in triumphal majesty up the sacred way to the eternal gates with all the powers of evil bound as captives behind his chariot before the eyes of men and angels."

By the resurrection Christ administered another blow to Satan, again demonstrating His complete power over all the forces of evil and proving that life, not death, is the final word. By rising from the dead in the power of an endless life He robbed death of its sting and the grave of its victory (1 Cor 15:55). Forty days later He ascended on high

(Heb 1:3), far above all "rule and authority and power and dominion" (Eph 1:21).

Before Christ took His final departure, He commanded His disciples to go into all the world, to preach the gospel to every creature, and to make disciples of all nations. Those were fighting words. They were tantamount to a declaration of war on Satan, who, though a defeated foe in the purpose of God, is nevertheless still very much alive and active in the world. For the time being, this world is still occupied territory and Satan is still its god and prince; but his power over the Christian has been broken, and the day will come when his kingdom will be completely destroyed, when Christ comes again to set up His kingdom here on the earth.

After 40 years I still remember a hymn we used to sing in China.

> To Thee, and to Thy Christ, O God,
>   We sing, we ever sing;
> For He hath crushed beneath His rod
>   The world's proud rebel king.
> He plunged in His imperial strength
>   To gulfs of darkness down;
> He brought His trophy up at length,
>   The foiled usurper's crown.

Man, the Creature, Cultivator, and Corrupter

Genesis 1 teaches that man came along as the climax of God's creative activity. Having created all the other creatures, God said, "Let us make man in our own image, according to our likeness." And He did just that. "God created man in His own image, in the image of God He created him; male and female He created them" (Gen 1:27).

The details are given in Genesis 2. God formed man's body out of the dust of the ground. Then he embraced the lifeless form and breathed into it the breath of life; and man became a living soul—different in kind as well as degree from all the other creatures that God made.

It was God's intention that man should be His vicar on earth. To this end He gave him authority over the birds of the air, the fish of the sea, and the beasts of the field. In a word, God honored man by sharing with him a little of His sovereignty. Man was to be supreme on the earth. God said to Adam, in effect, "All these creatures are to be subject to you. You will be subject to Me." And to spell out the limitations of man's autonomy, God placed upon Adam one solitary prohibition. There were hundreds of trees in the garden. Only one was off bounds. Of that tree he must not eat. If he did, he would die.

Not only did God invest man with authority, but He gave him responsibility as well. God knew that man needs both if he is to achieve maturity. Authority without responsibility leads to oppression. Responsibility without authority produces frustration. Consequently, God placed man in the garden with instructions to cultivate it.

We should note the cooperation here between the divine and the human. God created the garden and all the trees in it. That was a miracle. But it never was God's intention to *cultivate* the garden. That was something man could do, and God would require him to do his part. So we have two things here—the miracle and the mandate, God being responsible for the first, and man being responsible for the second.

Alas, we know how man behaved. With his eyes wide open, Adam partook of the forbidden fruit, and thereby introduced chaos into the garden. Instead of bringing forth fruits and flowers, it began to produce thorns and thistles; it has been doing so ever since. Thus man, by his disobedience, has, through history, turned his "garden" into a "ghetto."

From that day to this, man has gone from bad to worse—from cultivating the garden to corrupting it; from conserving its resources to exploiting them; from cooperating with his fellow man to competing with him; from preserving life to destroying life; from sharing to hoarding; from loving to hating. Man the cultivator became man the corrupter.

So corrupt did man become that by the time of the Flood he had reached the end of the rope and God had to act in judgment in an effort to bring man back to his senses. The antediluvian world had two outstanding characteristics— violence and corruption. "The earth," so goes the record, "was corrupt in the sight of God, and the earth was filled with violence. And God looked on the earth, and behold, it was corrupt; for all flesh had corrupted their way upon the earth" (Gen 6:11–12).

Corruption and violence go together. Corruption never exists alone. It always produces violence. Corruption takes many forms—personal, domestic, communal, but it always involves a breakdown of justice; and injustice, by its very nature, manifests itself in violence. One person gets more than his fair share, or he gets it by foul means. This stirs up jealousy, jealousy leads to opposition, and opposition ends in violence. In our society, the Mafia is a classic example.

Exploitation is part and parcel of man's inhumanity to man. The large gobble up the small. The rich exploit the poor. The strong oppress the weak. This is true of individuals, corporations, and governments. The tendency to exploit is universal. It is found in its most extreme form in the West, but it is by no means confined to the West. Businessmen in other parts of the world, given the opportunity, are guilty of the same behavior.

Here in our affluent society, the pursuit of the almighty dollar is well-nigh universal. The bottom line is always profit. The manner and extent to which we have used and misused our natural resources is a national scandal. Not only have we squandered our resources, but in the process we have polluted our rivers and lakes and contaminated the air in our great industrial centers.

Left to themselves, the industrialists will never clean

up the environment—it costs too much! So Congress has to pass laws to force compliance. Even then, there are evaders who circumvent the laws and literally get away with murder.

A classic example is strip-mining in the Appalachian Mountains. The big coal companies went in and extracted the coal by the cheapest methods. When they got what they wanted, they pulled out, leaving huge, ugly scars on the landscape and blighted lives in human communities. And we still haven't learned our lesson. We continue to consume our resources, some of them irreplaceable, with a voracious appetite. If something isn't done, we may well run out of some basic resources sometime in the twenty-first century. But we don't seem to care. We live for the present and let the future take care of itself. The price that our grandchildren will have to pay for our folly staggers the imagination.

As we have already noted, when God made man He placed him in a garden. When Cain went out angry from the presence of the Lord he built himself a city. Today God's handiwork is seen mostly in the country; alas, man's handiwork is all too evident in the city. And what a contrast there is between the two. We sing about the "alabaster cities" which "shine undimmed by human tears" but it has not worked out that way.

For the most part our large cities are a monument to the innate selfishness of human nature. They are indeed filled with violence and corruption. The streets are filthy; the alleys are piled high with garbage; the parks are littered with paper. The poor live in rat-infested houses owned, but not maintained, by absentee landlords. When they can't pay their rent, they are evicted without mercy. The unemployment rate in the inner city runs as high as 40 percent. Many of the mothers are trying to work and look after fatherless children at the same time. Trigger-happy street gangs roam the streets on the watch for any "enemy" that invades their turf. Most doors have two or three locks and even then homes are not always safe. Respectable people don't venture onto the streets after dark unless it is absolutely necessary. A friend of mine has lived on the near north side of Chicago for 17 years and never once ventured out after dark. Who can blame her? Last year more than nine hundred murders occurred in the city.

It is common knowledge that many of our big cities are threatened by gangsters. The Mafia has infiltrated politics, business, and labor, with the result that an increasing number of major transactions cannot be completed without some kind of payoff. Our streets are concrete jungles. Our schools have to be patrolled by armed police to protect the teachers from violence. Drug pushers, with their deadly wares, move about during school hours with impunity; so much so that the drug traffic threatens to undermine the public school system of the country. Tens of thousands of parents are taking their children out of the public schools and sending them to private schools to ensure a decent education.

Even high-minded people, interested in cleaning up the environment, often leave a mess behind them when they hold a meeting. I remember one night-long teach-in at Northwestern University in the seventies, addressed by a number of outstanding ecologists and attended by more than 1,500 students. The next morning, when it was all over, the sanitation crew was called in to clean up the mess. Chairs, tables, platform, and floor were littered with cigarette butts, beer cans, and coffee cups!

Why does man defile everything he touches? *Because he himself is defiled.* The Fall introduced chaos into every part of man's constitution—mind, heart, soul, and will. In a word, man is the victim of total depravity. Jesus reminded those who were concerned with external cleanliness that the real problem goes deeper. It is located in the heart. He said, "Hear, and understand. Not what enters into the mouth defiles the man, but what proceeds out of the mouth, this defiles the man. . . . The things that proceed out of the mouth come from the heart, and those defile the man. For out of the heart come evil thoughts, murders, adulteries, fornications, thefts, false witness, slanders. These are the things which defile the man" (Mt 15:10–11, 18–20).

The ultimate expression of corruption and violence is to be found in the empires of history. Every great empire was founded and maintained by force. Only when that force, for whatever reason, failed, did the empire fall. And along with political power went economic exploitation. This was especially true of the greatest empire of modern times— the British Empire. In the beginning, Great Britain was more interested in trade than power. She bought opium in India and sold it in China for a handsome profit.

Through the years the opium trade had devastating effects on China. Besides ruining the country economically, it destroyed the people physically. The patient Chinese endured the nefarious traffic until their patience ran out, whereupon they destroyed 20,000 chests of opium at Canton. That led to war—the Opium War, 1839–42 — which Gladstone described as "the blackest chapter in British history."

Both corruption and violence carry the seeds of their own destruction. No man or nation will long endure injustice. Sooner or later, the worm will turn and violence will break out. When Jesus declared that they that take the sword will perish by the sword, he pronounced doom on every empire founded on force.

In our own day we have seen how the moral law of cause and effect operates in the modern world. Following the Yom Kippur War in October 1973, the oil-producing countries of the Middle East threatened to cut off their supply of oil to the West. In the ensuing years they raised the price of oil some 400 percent, and we shouted foul play. But that is exactly the kind of game we had been playing for centuries. Our multinational corporations are still driving hard bargains all around the world.

Much of the violence in the Third World today is due more to economics than to politics. The rich are in favor of the status quo. The poor, on the other hand, are determined to overthrow the status quo and establish a government more responsive to their needs. And the bloodshed will continue until some degree of justice is achieved.

As I write this, the various religious factions in Lebanon are trying desperately to work out some modus operandi whereby they can live together in peace; but as long as the Christians, now in the minority, insist on holding on to power granted to them 40 years ago, there will be no lasting peace—just a succession of truces to be broken almost as soon as they are arranged. Again, it is a matter of justice. Without justice there can be no lasting peace.

God, the Creator, Ruler, and Redeemer

The Bible opens with the magnificent declaration: "In the beginning God created the heavens and the earth." If that were the only statement we had, it would be enough to establish God's ownership of the world.

In the West today there are two major views of the origin of the world—evolution and creation. One is the teaching of Scripture; the other is a theory advanced by a majority of scientists. I have always found it difficult to understand how anyone can accept the theory of evolution. If I were not a Christian, I would still have trouble with the theory of evolution. The tax on my credulity is just too great. I simply cannot believe that anything as incredibly complex as the universe can be the result of blind forces.

As far as the Bible is concerned, matter is not eternal, nor is the universe the result of electrical impulses or mechanical forces operating on their own, completely devoid of any plan or purpose. Whether we examine the nucleus of the atom or study the stars in their courses, we come to the same conclusion: "The hand that made us is divine."

Not only did God create the world, but He also owns it and is guiding it according to His own good purpose.

In [His] hand are the depths of the earth;
The peaks of the mountains are His also.
The sea is His, for it was He who made it;
And His hands formed the dry land. [Ps 95:4–5]

He also controls and sustains it (Is 40:28). Needless to say, He has a plan and a purpose for the world.

God is also the moral ruler of the world. The Scriptures portray God as a moral being, whose outstanding characteristic is holiness. To Israel He said, "I the LORD your God am holy" (Lev 19:2). Moreover, He demands holiness in His people (1 Pet 1:16). Indeed, without holiness no man will see the Lord (Heb 12:14).

Certain laws have been built into the fabric of the physical universe, and these cannot be broken without peril. Likewise, certain laws have been built into the fabric of the moral universe, and these are just as inexorable in their outworking as are the physical laws. No one can escape from the consequences of his wrongdoing. Man is a free moral agent and may sin if he chooses, but he cannot sin with impunity. "Be sure your sin will find you out" was God's word to Israel (Num 32:23). Again we read: "The soul that sinneth, it shall die" (Ez 18:4, KJV).

Sin always exposes the one who commits it to the judgment of God. This goes for cities and nations as well as individuals, since they too belong to God and come under His judgment. When the iniquity of the Amorites was full, judgment would fall (Gen 15:16). When the moral decadence of Sodom and Gomorrah reached unprecedented heights, they were destroyed with fire and brimstone (Gen 19). Nineveh barely escaped destruction by repenting at the preaching of Jonah. When the postdiluvians disobeyed God's command to replenish the earth, and instead built the Tower of Babel, God confounded their language. In the resulting confusion they went their separate ways and soon found themselves scattered over the face of the earth.

As people continued to wander farther and farther from God, they lost their knowledge of Him and became idolaters. However, their rejection of God in no way removed them from His rule. Even as "heathen" nations, with their false gods and sinful practices, they were still under God's universal control. They belonged to Him and were accountable to Him whether or not they acknowledged the fact.

The rule of God, then, extends to the ends of the earth. "The Lord has established His throne in the heavens; and His sovereignty rules over all" (Ps 103:19). "The earth is the LORD's, and all it contains, the world and those who dwell in it" (Ps 24:1). Psalm 47 is very clear on this point: "For the LORD Most High is to be feared, a great King over all the earth" (v. 2), and "God reigns over the nations" (v. 8).

If we were to read only the daily newspapers or listen only to the evening news we might easily get the impression that God has abdicated and that some monster of iniquity has climbed onto the throne, and the world is rushing pell mell to destruction. Such is not the case. God has no intentions of abdicating. He knows the end from the beginning, and is working all things after the counsel of His own sovereign will. He has a plan and a purpose for the church and the world, for the Jew and the Gentile; and when it is all over His purpose will be realized.

In addition to teaching that God is the creator and ruler of the world, the Bible also portrays God as its redeemer. Satan, as we have already seen, entered the Garden of Eden for the express purpose of destroying God's handiwork here on the earth. When Adam and Eve sinned, they joined Satan in his diabolical scheme. From that day to this, wherever man has gone, sin has run rampant. And it often appears as though God is either unable or unwilling to correct the situation. In reality, however, God's intention is to restore the world that has been blinded and blighted by sin and Satan.

God, through Isaiah, sought to comfort Israel in her distress with these words:

> Thus says the LORD, your creator, O Jacob,
> And He who formed you, O Israel,
> "Do not fear, for I have redeemed you;
> I have called you by name; you are Mine!" [Is 43:1]

In the same chapter (v. 3) He says, "I am the LORD your God, the Holy One of Israel, your Saviour."

It was never God's intention to allow sin to prevail to the end of time. Long before the creation of the world, long before the fall of man, God devised a plan for the ultimate restoration of the world. At the heart of that plan was the cross of Christ. In spite of its being filled with violence and corruption, this world has always been the object of God's love. Jesus told us, "God so loved the world, that He gave His only begotten Son, that whoever believes in Him should not perish, but have eternal life" (Jn 3:16). John said, "The Father has sent the Son to be the Savior of the world" (1 Jn 4:14). Paul said, "God was in Christ reconciling the world to Himself" (2 Cor 5:19).

Even in her idolatry and apostasy, Israel was never abandoned by God. Time and again He sent messengers to call Israel back to Himself—under the theocracy, the monarchy, and the captivity. He always wanted to do His people good. His word was:

> Let the wicked forsake his way,
> And the unrighteous man his thoughts;
> And let him return to the LORD,
> And He will have compassion on him;
> And to our God,
> For He will abundantly pardon. [Is 55:7]

We turn to the New Testament and discover that in the fullness of time God sent His Son (Gal 4:4). The Incarnation was God's idea, not man's. Time and again Christ reminded His hearers that He did not come of His own volition. He was sent by the Father for the salvation of the world. Jesus came as the supreme expression of God's concern for a fallen world, and He demonstrated that concern in word and deed. Peter summed it up in one sentence: "He went about doing good, and healing all who were oppressed by the devil; for God was with Him" (Acts 10:38). The climax came at the end of Jesus' life when He went to the cross and died—"the just for the unjust, in order that He might bring us to God" (1 Pet 3:18). We must adamantly reject the notion that the cross was Jesus' attempt to come between an outraged God and a sinful world. The cross was a demonstration of God's love (1 Jn 4:9–10). It was also the fulfillment of God's eternal purpose (Acts 4:27–28).

The Bible thus portrays God as a God of love whose heart goes out to the sinner and longs for his return. If the sinner rejects God's love and persists in his rebellion, God has to deal with him in judgment, but even then His act is an act of love. God's mighty acts are always redemptive in purpose, designed to show not only His creative power but also His redeeming grace. As for judgment, it is His "strange" work (Is 28:21, RSV). He takes no pleasure in the death of the wicked but desires rather that he should turn from his wicked way and live (Ez 33:11). When He finally resorts to judgment, it is to bring men and nations to their senses, to deliver them from self-destruction. In wrath He always remembers mercy (Hab 3:2).

In the coming of Christ, God acted decisively in human history. By His death and resurrection Christ disarmed the demonic power structures presided over by Satan. At the same time He delivered man from the law of sin and death. By so doing, He introduced a new order—the kingdom of God.

The idea of the kingdom was first introduced by John the Baptist, who came preaching the kingdom of God. "Repent," he said, "for the kingdom of heaven is at hand" (Mt 3:2). Jesus began His ministry saying the same thing: "The time is fulfilled, and the kingdom of God is at hand; repent and believe in the gospel" (Mk 1:15). In the person and preaching of Jesus, a new power entered human history. Matthew tells us that "Jesus was going about in all

Galilee, teaching in their synagogues, and proclaiming the gospel of the kingdom, and healing every kind of disease and every kind of sickness among the people" (Mt 4:23). In so doing He sought to destroy the works of the devil (1 Jn 3:8). Throughout His public ministry He clearly demonstrated His absolute power over man, nature, and demons, thus giving us a preview of what the coming kingdom was to involve.

The kingdom has appeared in the person and power of the King. The kingdom established by Christ is radically different from the kingdoms of this world (Jn 18:36). The kingdom, as defined by Christ, was to be an inner, spiritual kingdom (Lk 17:21), virtually closed to the worldly-wise (Mt 11:25) and the wealthy (Lk 18:25), but open to the meek (Mt 5:5), the poor (Lk 6:20), and even to the publicans and harlots, if they repented (Mt 21:32). It was to be spiritual in character (Rom 14:17), universal in scope (Mt 25:31–36), cosmopolitan in composition (Mt 8:11), and eternal in duration (Lk 1:33). It was to be founded on truth, not power (Jn 18:37); governed by love, not law (Rom 13:8–10); dedicated to peace, not war (Jn 18:33–38). Its rulers were to be servants, not lords (Mt 20:25–28). Its citizens were to be meek, merciful, pure, peaceful, and forgiving (Mt 5:5–11). Above all, they were to possess a new kind of righteousness, greater than that of the scribes and Pharisees (Mt 5:20).

Jesus was too realistic to think that this kind of rule could be established on a worldwide scale by unregenerate men. Only those who were "born again" or "born from above" could enter the kingdom of God (Jn 3:3). So He began with a handful of disciples. For three years He instructed them in the laws that were to govern His kingdom, and just before the Ascension He gave them their marching orders in the words of the Great Commission: "All authority has been given to Me in heaven and on earth. Go therefore and make disciples of all the nations, baptizing them in the name of the Father and the Son and the Holy Spirit, teaching them to observe all that I commanded you; and lo, I am with you always, even to the end of the age" (Mt 28:18–20).

This is what is known as the gospel mandate. It is important to note how it ties in with the cultural mandate given in Genesis. The command to Adam and Eve was: "Be fruitful and multiply, and fill the earth, and subdue it" (Gen 1:28). In this way, God planned to establish His rule over the whole earth. But before the mandate could be implemented, the Fall intervened, and the plan failed. In the Great Commission a second attempt is made to bring the world under the rule of God, this time not by physical procreation but by spiritual procreation. Now the command is: "Preach the gospel to every creature; make disciples of all nations."

The same idea comes out of God's commission to Paul, who was sent to the Gentiles "to open their eyes so that they may turn from darkness to light and from the dominion of Satan to God" (Acts 26:18). And converts, when they came along, were "delivered . . . from the domain of darkness, and transferred . . . to the kingdom of [God's] beloved Son" (Col 1:13).

Two of the seven parables in Matthew 13 were intended to describe the growth of the kingdom. The parable of the leaven (v. 33) obviously has to do with the penetration of Christianity into human society. The parable of the mustard seed (vv. 31–32) has to do with the geographical expansion of Christianity throughout the world. And we see both forces at work in the history of the church.

It was not long before the early Christians were scattered abroad, and they went everywhere preaching the gospel. They resided for the most part in the cities, where they lived their lives, reared their children, and plied their trades side by side with their pagan neighbors. Little by little, without fuss or fanfare, these simple, wholesome, joyous Christians made their presence felt and their secret known. The light was shining. The salt was penetrating. The leaven of the gospel was working its way through society.

One generation after Pentecost, Christian churches were found in all parts of the eastern half of the empire, so that Paul could write, "From Jerusalem and round about as far as Illyricum [modern-day Yugoslavia] I have fully preached the gospel of Christ" (Rom 15:19). Having evangelized the eastern part of the empire, he set his sights on Spain and hoped that the church in Rome would replace the church in Antioch as his base of operation.

By the year 200, the Christian presence had become so pervasive that Tertullian could write, "We are a new group but have already penetrated all areas of imperial life—cities, islands, villages, towns, market-places, even the camp, tribes, palaces, senate, the lawcourt. There is nothing left for you but your temples."[1]

Lest there be any doubt concerning the extension of God's rule over the world, Jesus declared, "This gospel of the kingdom shall be preached in the whole world for a witness to all the nations, and then the end shall come" (Mt 24:14).

With the coming of the Holy Spirit at Pentecost, the early disciples were given the kind of spiritual power required to live according to the laws of the kingdom laid down in the Sermon on the Mount. There is a sense, then, in which the church is the first fruits of the kingdom—the kingdom in embryonic form. In the church, the world should be able to see the kind of society God had intended from the very beginning, when He commanded Adam to multiply and subdue the earth.

The kingdom then is both present and future at the same time. It is here in microcosm. Its principles and powers are to be manifest in and through the church. Its full manifestation, however, will not be realized until the King returns in power and great glory to inaugurate the kingdom in person, at which time He will usher in a period of universal peace based on justice. Then the kingdoms of

---

1. Tertullian *Apology* 37.

the world will become the kingdom of our Lord and His
Christ, and He shall reign forever and ever (Rev 11:15).
In the meantime it is a fact—

> This is my Father's world,
> Oh, let me ne'er forget
> That though the wrong seems oft so strong,
> God is the ruler yet.
> This is my Father's world,
> Why should my heart be sad?
> The Lord is King, let the heavens ring,
> God reigns, let the earth be glad.

Both Isaiah (11:9) and Habakkuk (2:14) inform us that the
day is coming when the knowledge of the glory of God will
cover the earth as waters cover the sea. With this in mind,
Jesus taught His disciples to pray:

> "Our Father who art in heaven,
> Hallowed be Thy name.
> Thy kingdom come.
> Thy will be done,
> On earth as it is in heaven." [Mt 6:9–10]

PART 2

The Challenge
The World Mission We Must Face

4

Why I Believe in Christian Missions

T here are three good reasons for believing in Christian missions. Each one taken by itself is persuasive, but taken together they make a potent argument for the world mission of the Christian church.

I Believe in God

I believe not in any and every god, but in the God of the Bible, the God of Abraham, Isaac, and Jacob. The God and Father of Jesus Christ our Lord. I cannot believe in *that* God and not believe in Christian missions.

What kind of God is He? One cannot read the Scriptures, either the Old Testament or the New, and escape the conviction that the God of the Bible is a missionary God. It is a mistake to assume that Christian missions began with the Incarnation or Pentecost or any other event in history. The missionary enterprise is rooted in the very character of the God revealed in Scripture.

This is what Robert E. Speer had in mind when he wrote, "The supreme arguments for missions are not found in any specific words. It is in the very being and character of God that the deepest ground of the missionary enterprise is to be found. We cannot think of God except in terms which necessitate the missionary idea."[1]

To base the world mission of the Christian church solely on the Great Commission is to miss the whole thrust of biblical revelation. The missionary obligation of the church would have been just as imperative if Jesus had not spoken those words. The missionary mandate antedates the Incarnation and is rooted in the very character of God. Indeed, if Jehovah were not a missionary God, there would have been no Incarnation.

The two outstanding characteristics of God are love and holiness; both are essential to the concept of mission. From the pen of the apostle John we have two great declarations concerning God. One is that God is love (1 Jn 4:16); the other is that God is light (1 Jn 1:5).

God Is Love

God's questions to Adam were, "Where art thou? What hast thou done?" That is the heartcry of a God who has just lost His only son. In effect God said to Adam: All My plans for the world were riding on you. You were to be My vicar on earth, and to this end I gave you dominion over all living creatures. They were to be subject to you. You were to be subject only to Me. Now, you have failed Me. You have let Me down. You have frustrated My plans for the whole world. *What have you done?*

You see, man was created in the beginning not only by God but also *for* God, and God intended that man should find his highest happiness in Himself. Just as man *cannot* get along without God, so God *will not* get along without man. God then becomes the Hound of heaven. Once on the sinner's scent, He follows him to the end of the trail.

One does not get far into Genesis before discovering God's missionary concern. His remonstrance with Cain regarding the death of Abel (Gen 4), His solicitude for the

---

1. Robert E. Speer, *Christianity and the Nations* (New York: Revell, 1910), pp. 17–18.

safety of Noah and his family (Gen 6), His intervention at the tower of Babel (Gen 11), and His call to Abraham (Gen 12) are all evidences of God's concern for the safety, survival, and welfare of the human race.

Other biblical events with missionary overtones include Abraham's intercession for Sodom and Gomorrah (Gen 18), Joseph's influence in Egypt (Gen 42–47), Moses' part in the Exodus (Exod 1–12), Mordecai's intervention on behalf of the Jews doomed to genocide (Esther 1–10), Daniel's presence in the courts of Babylon and Medo-Persia (Dan 1–6), and Nehemiah's concern for the return of the captives (Neh 1–6).

And what shall we say concerning Jonah's mission to Nineveh? Nowhere is God's concern for the "heathen" more apparent than in the Book of Jonah. Jonah refused to go to Nineveh even to declare judgment on his enemies. Why? Because he knew full well that if the Ninevites repented, God in His abundant mercy would forgive and spare them. And this Jonah didn't want. Hence his rebellion. What Jonah feared, of course, is exactly what happened. Nineveh repented and God spared the city. God's judgments are intended to be remedial, not punitive. In wrath, He remembers mercy. He takes no pleasure in the death of the wicked. He desires that all men should turn from their wicked ways and accept His forgiveness.

His word through Isaiah was:

> Let the wicked forsake his way,
> And the unrighteous man his thoughts;
> And let him return to the Lord;
> And He will have compassion on him;
> And to our God,
> For He will abundantly pardon. [Is 55:7]

God loves the sinner with an everlasting love. And if the sinner remains recalcitrant to the end and finally goes to hell, even there he will be the object of God's love.

No one has expressed it more beautifully than Frederick W. Faber:

> There's a wideness in God's mercy
> Like the wideness of the sea;
> There's a kindness in His justice
> Which is more than liberty.
>
> For the love of God is broader
> Than the measure of man's mind;
> And the heart of the Eternal
> Is most wonderfully kind.

The ultimate expression of God's concern for lost humanity was the gift of His only Son. We have become so familiar with John 3:16 that its awesome significance has escaped us. It is an amazing thought that God so loved the world that He gave His only Son for the sins of the world. Jesus died, says Peter, "the just for the unjust, in order that He might bring us to God" (1 Pet 3:18). Paul says, "God was in Christ reconciling the world to Himself" (2 Cor 5:19).

The story is told of a rebellious girl in the Midwest who left home to get away from the restraints of home life. The mother, unable to contact her daughter, thought of an idea to attract the attention of the wayward girl. She took a photograph of herself, wrote across its face the two words *come home,* and placed it in the window of the corner drugstore. One day, after weeks of fruitless search for pleasure, the girl passed the store, and there in the window noticed the picture of her mother. Looking more closely she saw the familiar handwriting—"Come Home." Bidding farewell to her companions, she returned home to receive a warm welcome from her mother.

It seems to me that the four Gospels, with their beautiful story of Jesus and His matchless life of perfect love, can be seen as a photograph of God set down in the window of the world, over the face of which we can see, written by the finger of God, the two beautiful words *come home.*

How can anyone believe in that kind of God and not believe in Christian missions?

God Is Light

The second great attribute of God revealed in the Scriptures is holiness. "God is light, and in Him there is no darkness at all" (1 Jn 1:5). The term *light*, of course, is symbolic and is used in three ways in the Bible. It refers to physical glory or splendor (2 Cor 4:6; Rev 21:23), intellectual truth (Ps 43:3), and moral holiness (Rom 13:11–14).

Everything pertaining to God speaks of the beauty of holiness. His law is perfect (Ps 19:7). His commandment is holy and just and good (Rom 7:12). His throne is a throne of holiness (Ps 47:8). His kingdom is a kingdom of righteousness (Mt 6:33). His scepter is a scepter of equity (Ps 45:6). The psalmist summed it all up in one sentence when he spoke of Jehovah as being righteous in all His ways and holy in all His works (Ps 145:17).

Associated with God's holiness is His wrath, which is revealed from heaven against "all ungodliness and unrighteousness of men" (Rom 1:18). If man rejects God's love—and some do—he shuts himself up to God's wrath. We tend to place these two attributes, love and wrath, in separate compartments. His love, we assume, is reserved for His children; His wrath for His enemies. Not so. His love and wrath cannot be separated in this fashion. They are not two entities; rather they are two aspects of one entity—His holiness. His holiness glows with love; His love burns with holiness. He cannot express the one without, at the same time, expressing the other. If God is going to save the sinner He must do so in a way that does not violate His holiness.

God loves the sinner at the same time that He hates his sin. He loves righteousness *and* hates iniquity (Heb 1:9). The one is the corollary of the other. To love righteousness *is* to hate iniquity. This must be true in the very nature of the case. There is, therefore, no incompatibility between

God's love and His wrath. His just wrath is an expression of His holy love.

If God were only love and not light, there would be no need of the Christian mission. He could save all men by a word, without faith or repentance. In that case there would be no need to preach the gospel. But Paul knew better. He declared, "Therefore knowing the fear of the Lord, we persuade men" (2 Cor 5:11). He also said, "Woe is me if I do not preach the gospel" (1 Cor 9:16). The love of God makes heaven possible. The holiness of God makes hell necessary.

The idea of everlasting punishment is totally unacceptable to the modern mind. Christians then have to choose between the modern mind and the mind of Christ. We do well to bear in mind that, after all, it was Christ who first taught this awful doctrine. The word *gehenna* (hell) occurs 12 times in the New Testament; 11 times it came from the lips of Christ. If we accept what Jesus said about heaven, we can hardly reject what He said about hell. If He was an authority on the one, He was an authority on the other. The awful words about "the unquenchable fire," "the worm that dieth not," and "weeping and gnashing of teeth" are not the wild, irresponsible words of some fiery evangelist trying to scare sinners into the kingdom. These words, terrible as they are, fell from the lips of the meekest man who ever lived, the Friend of publicans and sinners, the Man who gave His life and shed His blood that men might be forgiven. And they were spoken, we may be sure, with a tear in His eye and a quiver in His voice.

The age-old question is: How can sinful man stand in the presence of a holy God?

> Eternal Light, eternal Light,
>   How pure the soul must be
> When placed within Thy searching sight
> It shrinks not but with calm delight
>   Can live and look on Thee.
>
> The spirits that surround Thy throne
>   May bear the burning bliss;

> But that is surely theirs alone
> For they have never, never known
> A fallen world like this.
>
> Oh how shall I whose native sphere
> Is dark, whose mind is dim,
> Before the Ineffable appear
> And on my naked spirit bear
> The uncreated beam?

Left to himself, man has no answer to that agonizing question. But God has not left man to himself. He has come to him in the Incarnation. Consequently, there is hope.

> There is a way for man to rise
> To that sublime abode;
> An offering and a sacrifice,
> A Holy Spirit's energies,
> An Advocate with God.
>
> These, these prepare us for the sight
> Of holiness above;
> The sons of ignorance and night
> May dwell in the eternal Light
> Through the eternal Love.

Yes, God is a missionary God. The human race is His family. The world, with all its faults and flaws, is His world. He created it in the beginning. He has sustained all these millions—or billions—of years; and He intends to save it. To this end, He sent His Son, who lived, died, and rose again that He might be the Savior of the world. And God will never be satisfied until every member of the human race is given an opportunity to accept or reject Jesus Christ.

I Believe in Christ

How can anyone be a follower of Karl Marx and not believe in world revolution? How can anyone be a protégé

of Martin Luther King and not believe in civil rights? In
like manner, how can anyone be a follower of Jesus Christ
and not believe in Christian missions?

The world mission of the Christian church goes back to
Pentecost. Indeed, it antedates Pentecost. It was launched
by Christ Himself. He was the first and greatest missionary. In Hebrews 3:1 Christ is referred to as the "Apostle
and High Priest of our confession." The word *apostle* has
the same meaning as the noun *missionary*. One is derived
from the Greek; the other comes from Latin. But they both
mean "one who is sent."

Time and again, in the Gospel of John, Jesus insisted
that His mission to this world was not His idea but God's.
He was sent by the Father (Jn 6:57), to do the Father's will
(Jn 6:38), to speak the Father's words (Jn 12:49), to do the
Father's works (Jn 5:19). He was the "Sent One"—the missionary. But He was no ordinary missionary. He was the
Missionary Extraordinary. He came not so much to proclaim salvation as to provide it. And this He did by His
atoning death and victorious resurrection. The apostle
John summed it up in one sentence: "The Father has sent
the Son to be the Savior of the world" (1 Jn 4:14).

The church's mission is but an extension of Christ's mission. Said Jesus, "As the Father has sent Me, I also send
you" (Jn 20:21). As God became incarnate in Christ in
order to provide salvation for the world, so the Holy Spirit
became incarnate in the church in order to proclaim salvation to the ends of the earth.

It is difficult to study the life and teachings of Christ and
escape the conviction that He intended His redemptive
mission to be continued and consummated by His followers. In the early part of His public ministry He confined
His efforts largely to the Jewish people. This was only
right and proper in view of the fact that He was their
Messiah foretold by the Old Testament prophets. His first
offer of the kingdom must of necessity be made to the Jews;
but when they refused both Him and the kingdom, He had
no choice but to address His appeal to the Gentiles as well.

But even before He turned to the Gentiles, there are intimations of a worldwide ministry. In His first sermon in the synagogue in Nazareth, He incurred the wrath of His compatriots by making honorable mention of two Gentiles in the Old Testament (Lk 4:16–30). Early in His ministry He warned that Gentiles with faith are better off than Jews without faith; He went on to say that many would come from the east and west, and sit down with Abraham, Isaac, and Jacob in the kingdom of God, while the children of the kingdom (the Jews) would be cast out (Mt 8:11–12).

It seems clear from the Gospel of John that Jesus perceived His mission in worldwide terms. The word *kosmos* (world) is used 79 times, mostly by Jesus Himself. The opening verses set the tone for the entire book. "He was in the world, and the world was made through Him, and the world did not know Him" (Jn 1:10). John the Baptist points Him out as the "Lamb of God who takes away the sin of the world" (Jn 1:29). The Samaritans acknowledge Him not as the Messiah of Israel but as the Savior of the world (Jn 4:42).

Equally clear are the teachings of Christ. He claimed to be the "bread of life" that He would give for the life of the world (Jn 8:12). He claimed that if He were lifted up He would draw all men to Himself (Jn 12:32). While offering the kingdom to the Jews, He refused to restrict His ministry to them. He lived in Galilee of the Gentiles. He ministered in despised Samaria. He visited the cities of the Decapolis beyond Jordan. He healed the daughter of the Syrophoenician woman, did the same for the centurion's slave, and shared the water of life with the outcast woman of Samaria. He declared that the field is the world, not Palestine or even the Roman Empire.

The turning point came after the Resurrection. With universal salvation procured by His death and resurrection, Jesus then no longer speaks in narrow nationalistic terms. He is now free to reveal His real and ultimate purpose—the salvation of the world. During the 40 days between the Resurrection and Pentecost Jesus gave His apostles further instructions regarding the kingdom of God (Acts 1:3). The kingdom was not to be restricted to Israel. Nor was it to be an earthly kingdom based on temporal power. It was to be a new kind of kingdom—based on truth, governed by love, and dedicated to peace. It was to be established first in the hearts of His followers and they were to extend it to the ends of the earth by the worldwide proclamation of the gospel.

Just before Jesus left His apostles for the last time He called them together and gave them their marching orders for all time to come. They had been with Him for three years. They had witnessed every miracle. They had listened to every important message. They had seen Him under various circumstances. They knew Him better than anyone else did. They had received His words; they knew His plans; they shared His hopes. Such high privilege, however, brought with it heavy responsibility. Now they were to go into all the world, preach the gospel to every creature, and make disciples of all nations (Mt 28:19–20). How can anyone be a follower of this Man and not believe in Christian missions?

This is not to say that everyone is called to be a full-time missionary. Obviously, that is both unnecessary and undesirable. But every follower of Christ is expected to have a deep, personal interest in and ongoing commitment to Christian missions. The few who go and the many who remain at home to support them are all part of one team. Both are equally important to the cause of missions at home and abroad.

Missionary work is the most magnanimous form of humanitarian service. It requires a large heart not only on the part of the missionary but also on the part of supporters at home. By and large, these supporters have not been very generous. Jesus said, "It is more blessed to give than to receive" (Acts 20:35). Few Christians really believe that statement, at least if their actions are any criterion. Last year the average church member in the United States gave less than 50 cents a week to home and foreign missions.

Again, Jesus said, "Freely you received, freely give" (Mt 10:8). This is precisely what He did. He was always on the giving end. He gave unstintingly of His love, grace, time, and strength. His interest went far beyond the small circle of His friends and followers. He came to save the world (Jn 3:17), not just the church. Hence, He ministered to all and sundry—Gentiles as well as Jews, poor as well as rich, wicked as well as righteous. Indeed, He seemed to have a special compassion for those who had been bypassed by the crowd or cast off by society. On one occasion, when criticized for fraternizing with the publicans and sinners, He defended His conduct by saying, "It is not those who are healthy who need a physician, but those who are ill. . . . I did not come to call the righteous, but sinners" (Mt 9:12–13).

Jesus has been described as the "man for others." Indeed, He was just that. He worked for others. He lived for others. He died for others. He had time for everyone—Nicodemus, Zacchaeus, Bartimaeus, Mary Magdalene, the woman of Samaria, the Syrophoenician woman, the Roman centurion, and the thief on the cross. Even the little children found a welcome, over the protests of the disciples who thought to protect Jesus from too many distractions.

Peter summed it all up in one sentence: "He went about doing good" (Acts 10:38). Paul said, "[He] loved me, and delivered Himself up for me" (Gal 2:20). He spent His entire public ministry teaching, preaching, helping, healing. He Himself stated that He had come not to be ministered to, but to minister and to give His life a ransom for many (Mt 20:28). And at the close of His life He went to the cross and died, the just for the unjust, to bring us to God (1 Pet 3:18).

It is instructive to note that His last miracle, before going to the cross, was an act of healing, when He restored the ear of an enemy which Peter had severed in his vain attempt to save Jesus from arrest. With Jesus, "doing good" was not simply part of His messianic mission; it was an expression of His loving, caring nature. For this reason, He never failed to respond to human need, regardless of what the need was.

In so doing, He placed every follower under obligation to do the same. Every disciple must follow in the steps of the Master. He lived for others; so must the disciple. Whether a Christian ever becomes a full-time missionary is beside the point. The issue is: Does he believe in missions—*really* believe? Is missions his *first* love? Does he seek *first* the kingdom of God or do other things come first—business, pleasure, profession, advancement, achievement? What place does world missions have on his agenda? Is it at the top, the bottom, or somewhere in between?

To be a follower of Christ and not be a World Christian is a contradiction in terms. Christ is the world's Savior. His followers must be World Christians.

I Believe in Man

At first glance this seems like a strange thing to say. Knowing the state of the world today, how can anyone say he believes in man? Does the Bible not say that man is in bondage to sin and Satan, deceitful, deceived, serving diverse lusts and pleasures, living in malice and envy, hateful and hating others? Did God not despair of man in the days of Noah? Did not even Israel disappoint God and lapse into idolatry time after time? Did not the Gentile world abandon the knowledge of God and turn the glory of God into an image like unto man, birds, beasts, and creeping things? Did God not say that the heart of man is incurably wicked? How then can you believe in man?

It is true that man is lost, willfully and hopelessly lost. Nor is that all. He has no desire to repent and go straight. He has lived so long in a state of sin that he has become naturalized in the unnatural to the point where he actually loves darkness rather than light. He has gone astray, not like a bird but like a sheep, with no homing instinct.

Left to himself he will always travel the downward road, farther and farther from God. How then can you say you believe in man? Is he not hopeless and as well helpless? Helpless, yes; hopeless, no.

I believe in man not because of what he is but because of what, by the grace of God and the power of the gospel, he may become. This comes out most clearly in the ministry of Christ. He changed every life He touched. Before she met Jesus, Mary Magdalene was a wild-eyed, demon-possessed woman of the street. After she met Jesus, she was His most devoted follower, one of the last at the cross and the first at the empty tomb. Before he met Jesus, Zacchaeus was an unscrupulous tax collector who had used his office to enrich himself at the expense of others. After he met Jesus, he said, "Behold, Lord, half of my possessions I will give to the poor, and if I have defrauded anyone of anything, I will give back four times as much" (Lk 19:8). That's real conversion! Jesus replied, "Today salvation has come to this house."

Before he met Jesus, Saul of Tarsus was the head of the Gestapo in Jerusalem, only instead of killing Jews, he killed Christians—hundreds of them. And when he had rounded up all the Christians in Jerusalem, he moved on to other cities with the same intent. After he met Jesus on the Damascus road, he became the greatest of all the apostles and spent the remainder of his life building the things he once destroyed. And the life-changing power of the gospel is seen in the missionary movement of our day.

Salvation has been defined as the power of God working in the heart of man to undo all the chaos introduced into the life and constitution of man by the Fall. The divine image in man has been badly damaged but not completely destroyed. Had it been destroyed, man would be beyond redemption. The mind of man has been darkened by sin and Satan, but he still retains a consciousness of God to which the gospel can appeal.

At the time of the Fall the virus of sin invaded every part of man's constitution. His mind was darkened. His emotions were vitiated. His will was enslaved. Even his body came under the sentence of death. The whole purpose of redemption is to restore man to what he was when he came from the hand of God. This is what Jesus had in mind when he asked, "Will you be made whole?" The word *whole* comes from the Anglo Saxon root, "hal," from which we also get the words *health* and *holiness*. Just as man's body was made for health, not disease, so his heart and mind were made for holiness, not sin. To be "made whole" means more than the healing of the body. It includes the healing of the soul as well. Jesus' first words to the paralytic were: "My son, your sins are forgiven" (Mk 2:5). Later on, he added, "Take up your pallet and go home" (v. 11). Salvation is much more than the salvation of the soul. It includes as well the redemption of body and spirit—in short, it includes the entire man.

The whole thrust of Christian missions is nothing short of the salvation of the world—beginning with the individual and extending to the institutions and structures of society. Salvation is first personal and then societal. Jesus taught: "Thou shalt love the Lord thy God with all thy heart, and with all thy soul, and with all thy mind. . . . Thou shalt love thy neighbour as thyself" (Mt 22:37, 39, KJV). The gospel, then, has social as well as personal implications. And wherever the gospel has been preached it has changed individuals and sometimes whole communities.

Thirty years ago, for example, the gospel was first introduced into the Baliem Valley of Irian Jaya. At that time the inhabitants were just emerging from the Stone Age. The first Dani tribesman to greet the missionaries carried spears, stone-headed battle axes, and bows and arrows. The missionaries didn't know whether the reception would be friendly or hostile. Pioneer missionaries in other parts of Irian Jaya had been murdered. Today the Baliem Valley, 40 miles long and 10 miles wide, is dotted with 150 churches and preaching points led by nationals. Some 25,000 Danis—one-third of the entire tribe—are Christians. These churches are self-supporting and even are supporting their own missionaries to other tribes. And all this has taken place in a single generation.

About the turn of the century Christian missionaries began work among the head-hunting tribal peoples of Northeast India. Today the Kukis, the Nagas, and the Mizos are almost 100 percent Christian with their own churches, schools, hospitals, and other humanitarian institutions. One of these Christians is Rochunga Pudiate, general director of Bibles for the World, Inc., in Wheaton, Illinois, an organization that has distributed millions of copies of the Scriptures in various countries of the world. His biography, *God's Tribesman,* has been written by James and Marti Hefley.

Other books dealing with the transformation of pagan societies include *Wind through the Bamboo* by Donna Strom, *Peace Child* by Don Richardson, *Cannibal Valley* by Russell T. Hitt, and *God's City in the Jungle* by Sanna Barlow Rossi. The December 27, 1982, issue of *Time* carried an excellent feature article on "The New Missionary."

The Christian mission operates in a broken world. That's where it does its best work. No person is so bound and broken by sin that he cannot be delivered from its power. No society is so depraved that it cannot be reclaimed. No culture is so corrupt that it cannot be purified.

When Jesus was here He preached the gospel, healed the sick, cleansed the leper, and raised the dead. When He sent out the Twelve He gave them power to do the same. The gospel is the most liberating message the world has ever heard. The Bible is the most revolutionary book mankind has ever read. A girl in a mission school in Africa, when asked what she knew about the Bible, said, "Oh, I know about the Bible. That's the book that begins with Genesis and ends with Revolutions." Indeed it does.

Wherever the gospel goes it makes bad men good and good men better. It is simply a matter of record that in many parts of the Third World, Christians are the most dynamic, most progressive segment of society. Their rate of literacy, their reputation for honesty, their desire to help others are usually higher than those of the rest of the community. When it comes to employment, they are often preferred to non-Christians because they are more industrious and more reliable. They are an altogether stable element in society. Even in the Peoples' Communes in China, the Christians were known for their hard work and honest toil, and as a result they were often given positions of responsibility.

The Christian mission, in the last decades of the twentieth century, affords ample evidence that the gospel is indeed the power of God unto salvation to everyone who believes. There are tens of millions of people in the Third World who are what they are today because the missionaries of the nineteenth and twentieth centuries took the gospel to them.

5

Why I Believe in Foreign Missions

I t has been customary in mission circles to divide the mission field into two major areas—home and foreign. The distinction serves a purpose, but we do well not to push the idea too far.

Let me make it quite plain. I believe in *home* missions. They are just as important as foreign missions. In fact, from some points of view, home missions are more difficult and sometimes more dangerous than foreign missions. Take, for instance, the ghettos in our large cities. Any pastor who leaves the green pastures of suburbia and moves his family into the inner city to pursue Christian work there is, by any definition, a missionary. In fact, he will be safer in Tokyo than in Chicago, and his children will receive a better education. So, I have no desire to denigrate home missions.

We should also bear in mind that the Bible makes no distinction between home and foreign missions. There are many "unreached peoples" in the United States. The field, said Jesus, is the world—the whole world—and no part of that world is "foreign" to Him. It is true that missions, like charity, begin at home; accordingly the apostles were instructed to start in Jerusalem, and from there proceed to Judea and Samaria, and finally to go to the ends of the earth.

If this is true, then why the emphasis on foreign missions? The answer is not that the need is greater on the foreign field. It is rather that there are fewer resources there to meet the need. When people say, as they sometimes do, "Why go overseas? we have plenty of heathen at home," they are in one sense making an important point. A human soul is just as precious in Boston as in Bangladesh, and to be "lost" in Milwaukee is just as fraught with peril as to be "lost" in Morocco.

That is true; but there is a significant difference. Anyone who is a "heathen" in the United States is a "heathen" by choice, whereas the billions in the Third World who have never heard the gospel are "heathen" by chance. In the United States there are ample resources to meet the spiritual needs of 240 million people, whereas on the foreign mission field the resources are meager, sometimes nonexistent.

We can see the extent of this difference when we consider several factors: the spiritual affluence of the West, the poverty of the Third World, the paucity of trained leaders overseas, and the magnitude of the unfinished task.

The Spiritual Affluence of the West

We Americans have enjoyed spiritual affluence so long that we have come to take it for granted! And this affluence extends to all phases of church life and work. In this country there are almost 300,000 evangelical churches. In addition there are some 32,000 evangelical Christian day schools, nine thousand evangelical bookstores, three thousand Christian summer camps, and more than three hundred Bible schools. There are more students enrolled in Moody Bible Institute than in all the Bible schools in Europe. And on and on it goes. The affluence is overwhelming.

In our country there are more preachers than policemen, more churches than schools. Year after year the Bible is the best seller. Indeed, in the last 30 years we have produced 40 different versions of the English Bible! We have more than a thousand Christian radio stations, most of them on the air seven days a week—some of them, 24 hours a day. In many cities on Sunday morning the airwaves are crowded with church services, most of them at the local level. Some radio preachers speak to more people in one week than the apostle Paul addressed in his lifetime. Now we have scores of Christian television stations in various parts of the country and one new one comes on the air each month. In addition, there are nationwide programs sponsored by the electronic church.

Many of these programs are sponsored by evangelicals and usually contain a gospel message. If the listener wants a copy of the message, he need only drop a post card in the mail and the message will be sent to him free and postage paid. If he wants a Bible and can't afford it, he can secure one from a dozen organizations dedicated to the distribution of the Scriptures. Last year the American Bible Society alone distributed 126,355,579 copies of the Scriptures here in the United States!

For blind people, the entire Bible is available in Braille. If that is too difficult, it can be ordered on tape. Bibles are found in most hotels. Each Days Inn has two Bibles in each room: one to be read and the other to be taken home free if the person so desires. Almost all the large denominations publish their own hymnals and Sunday-school materials. Other denominations, large and small, have their own house organs, geared to the needs and interests of their own parishioners. In addition, there are scores of non-denominational publishing houses, such as Scripture Press, Gospel Light, Moody, Eerdmans, and Zondervan.

Even persons cut off from the mainstream of American life have access to the gospel in one form or another. Young Americans being inducted into the armed services are presented with a New Testament by the Gideons; once in the service they have chaplains, Roman Catholic, Jewish, and Protestant, to minister to their spiritual needs. Even those who find themselves behind bars have chaplains and chapel services on the premises, and those who wish to do so can enroll free of charge in Bible correspondence courses from Moody Bible Institute.

It is a cause for general rejoicing when we are informed that *Good News for Modern Man* has sold more than 70 million copies since its first appearance in the mid-1960s, and that more than 30 million copies of the *Living Bible* have been sold since 1971. Our joy, however, is somewhat tarnished when we learn that the vast majority of these Scriptures were distributed right here in the United States.

Whenever a new version of the English Bible appears in this country, it is customary to have a promotional banquet in some large city such as Chicago, New York, or Los Angeles. Hundreds of local pastors and their wives are invited to these gatherings and are treated to a delicious dinner free of charge; at the close of the program each pastor is presented with a free copy of the new Bible. I have a friend who was given three different Bibles at a large gathering in Washington, D.C.

It is difficult to believe that any person in this country could not come to know the way of salvation within a week—if he or she were really interested.

The Poverty of the Third World

What is the condition of the churches in the Third World? How large are they? How strong are they—spiritually, financially, institutionally? Do they have all the resources needed to pay their own way, train their own clergy, maintain existing institutions, and at the same time reach out to the non-Christians who in some countries outnumber the Christians 10 or 20 to 1?

It is common knowledge that the church in any society finds it difficult to rise higher than the community in which it is located because its members usually represent a cross section of that society. Because most Third World countries are desperately poor, the churches in those countries tend likewise to be poor.

There are, of course, exceptions. The churches in Japan, Korea, Taiwan, Singapore, and Hong Kong compare favorably with the best churches in our country. This is especially true of Korea and Japan where the pastors are well trained and many of them are better paid than the missionaries.

Be it said to the glory of God and the credit of the early missionaries and present-day leaders that there are some large churches in nearly all parts of the world. The Anglicans have large churches in Nigeria, Kenya, and Tanzania; the Lutherans in Tanzania, Lesotho, and Indonesia; the Baptists in Burma, Brazil, Nigeria, and Zaire, the Presbyterians in Zaire, Malawi, Korea, and Ghana; the Methodists in India, Korea, Ghana, and Zimbabwe; the Pentecostals in Brazil, Chile, Kenya, Indonesia, and Korea. Church union in the Third World is way ahead of church union in the West. As a result there are some very large "united churches" in Japan, the Philippines, India, and Zaire. The faith missions have produced some large churches in Nigeria, Kenya, Vietnam, and other places, including China in pre-revolution days.

These churches, however, are the exception, not the rule. The other churches in the Third World tend to be weak and small, and to comprise people drawn mainly from the lower echelons of society. It stands to reason, if the annual per capita income in a given country is $300, the per capita income of the average church member would be about the same. If the country as a whole is poor, the church in that country is likely to be poor.

To make matters worse, women predominate in most Third World churches. The menfolk are too busy or they have no interest in religion, and they leave it up to the womenfolk to take care of the spiritual needs of the family. The women in these divided families, though they may wish to do so, are not always free to support the church. The husbands work hard for the money they make and are not happy when their wives want to use their meager income for the support of the church. Certainly they will not permit their women to tithe. As a result, most Third World churches are poor. Again, Japan is an exception.

The degree of the poverty of Third World churches can be seen in the fact that many churches cannot support a full-time pastor. In that case, the pastors must agree to serve with little or no financial remuneration. In Africa, for instance, many pastors receive no salary but are given a plot of ground that they till. In this way their basic needs are met. But little is left over for the good things of life that we take for granted. Pastors' families, like other families, tend to be large. To feed and clothe them is a perennial problem. To give them an adequate education is impossible.

According to Overseas Crusades, the average Filipino pastor sees only $10 cash per month. The rest of his income comes in the form of rice, corn, and pork from the church members. A major problem for his remaining in the pastorate is economic survival. In order to make ends meet, he must often take another job. The pastor's house has two or three rooms made of bamboo poles or palm branches with a thatched roof. If it is a "deluxe" model it will be made of used lumber or possibly cement block. The toilet is an outhouse. Of course, there is no running water or any of the other utilities. Churches are built the same way. The pews consist of two parallel bamboo poles supported by a couple of sawhorses. Often there are no hymnbooks, and parishioners must furnish their own Bibles.

A similar story is told by SIM International regarding its work in Bolivia.

Poverty is a usual state for too many of Bolivia's people, including evangelical Christians. The struggle for sustenance drains their meager resources, leaving them at the bottom of the development ladder. It is a relentless cycle in which poverty nurtures ignorance, and ignorance nur-

tures poverty. The effect of this on churches in poor communities is sad. Some congregations, mainly in rural areas
where population is sparse, are not much bigger than the
ten-baptized-members-in-good-standing minimum required by UCE for recognition as a properly constituted
church. Such a handful of people simply cannot support a
pastor or maintain more than the most elementary Christian education programs.[1]

In many parts of the world the Christians are so poor
that it is with great difficulty that they procure a copy of
the Scriptures. In spite of the fact that Bibles on the mission field are subsidized by the Bible societies, the price is
beyond the reach of many. It is not uncommon for an ar-
tisan to have to pay two or three days' wages for a New
Testament. Indeed, in some parts of the world there are
churches that are still waiting for their *first* copy of the
complete Bible. A recent letter from a friend of mine told
of a Bible school in Zaire where, on a test, the class was
asked to name the first book in the Bible. The answer came
back, "Matthew." Yes, Matthew is the first book in *their*
Bible.

The Paucity of Trained Leaders

Two generations ago John R. Mott stated that the greatest weakness of the missionary movement was our failure
to produce well-trained leaders for national churches.
Half a century has come and gone since then and the problem is still with us. In spite of all that has been said and
done in the intervening years, the churches in many parts
of the mission field are still without adequately trained
pastors and evangelists. Only three countries in Asia—
Japan, Korea, and Taiwan—have anything like an adequate number of well-trained pastors. In other parts of the

1. *SIM Now,* March/April 1982, p. 7.

world it is not uncommon to find a pastor who is responsible for the oversight of anywhere from 10 to 20 congregations. In Brazil alone, the Assemblies of God have 59,600 church leaders. Only 3,000 of them have had any formal theological education by extension.

One reason for this melancholy state of affairs is the phenomenal growth of the church in recent years, especially in Latin America and Black Africa. Hank Griffith, Evangelical Free missionary in Zaire, has this to say:

> Praise God for the numerical growth He has produced in the Evangelical Church of Ubangi! The number of adult church members has increased 60 percent in three years . . . and the number of churches 15 percent.
>
> However, only 15 percent of these 409 churches are pastored by Bible Institute graduates. Perhaps close to 35 percent of the churches have leaders with two years of low level Bible school. The remaining 50 percent are being led by sincere men of God who may or may not have had several Bible courses by extension or correspondence. Most of these men are doing the best they know, but they often do not know the role of the pastor.[2]

The situation in Black Africa has reached a critical stage. As a result of a vast influx of converts into the church, the number of churches has increased dramatically in recent years. Consequently there are not nearly enough leaders to go around. The demand far outstrips the supply. As a result we are achieving quantity at the expense of quality. The numerical growth is very gratifying, but the quality of leadership leaves much to be desired. If something is not done to correct the situation, all kinds of ethical and theological aberrations are likely to appear. Byang Kato, former executive director of the Association of Evangelicals of Africa and Madagascar, has warned that

2. *Prayer Letter,* September 1981.

the greatest danger facing the African church is Christo-paganism.

Many of the present-day pastors are older men—good, godly men—with a meager education. Their theological books could all be placed on a 12-inch-long shelf. Many of them do not possess a concordance or a Bible dictionary or more than one or two expository books. As for books on homiletics, apologetics, counseling, church administration, family planning, they simply don't exist. So the pastors have a hard time trying to prepare good, solid biblical sermons week after week. They depend largely on personal experiences, visions, dreams, or anecdotes, and soon run out of them. Then they have to start all over again. Fortunately, peoples in the Third World don't mind repetition. Even so, the net result is not very satisfactory.

Inadequately-trained pastors are at a serious disadvantage when called upon to minister in an urban setting. The city churches are attracting more and more high-school and college students and professional people. They are not going to be satisfied with messages that are completely lacking in intellectual content. They want something for the mind as well as the heart.

This being so, the greatest contribution that Western missionaries can make in Africa is not in the area of evangelism. The African Christians are doing a superb job in reaching their neighbors. What they desperately need is sound Bible teaching at all levels from Sunday school through seminary. Unfortunately, some missionaries think they must be out on the firing line of evangelism or else they have missed their calling.

In the whole of Black Africa there is only one evangelical seminary for all the 15 countries of Francophone Africa, and that seminary is hurting for lack of financial and other forms of support. One problem is that it is an interdenominational institution and no one mission or denomination feels any great sense of responsibility for its success.

Another seminary, designed to meet the expanding

needs of Anglophone Africa, has recently been established in Nairobi. It remains to be seen what support it can command.

Theological Education by Extension, which began in Guatemala in the early 1960s, is now functioning in all parts of the world and is meeting with widespread, enthusiastic support. TEE, as it is known, is designed to take the seminary to the student, rather than, in the traditional way, to have the student attend the seminary. The students work in their own time at their own pace. Several times a year the students meet in some central location with the seminary or Bible-college professor for counsel, encouragement, and direction, but not for instruction. The students are expected to study on their own with the use of specially prepared materials supplied by the school. TEE has become very popular. According to Lois McKinney of Wheaton Graduate School, the number of enrollees may be as high as 100,000.

The Unfinished Task of Evangelism

In spite of herculean efforts during the last two centuries, large areas of the world are still without the gospel of Christ. In fact, the number of Christians in the world is not keeping up with the population growth. Twenty-five years ago, Christians accounted for 33 percent of the world's population. Today the ratio is slightly below 30 percent. Much of that drop is due to the fact that population growth has tapered off in the so-called Christian countries, while a veritable population explosion has taken place in many parts of the Third World, especially in Africa and Latin America.

1. *Evangelism is a universal task.* We have been commanded by our Lord to go into *all* the world, to preach the gospel to *every* creature, and to make disciples of *all* nations. It is fair to ask: After two thousand years, how are

we doing? Are we forging ahead? Are we standing still? Or are we falling behind?

The population of the world stands today at about 4.8 billion. Of this number, some 1.4 billion adhere to some form of the Christian faith—Catholic, Orthodox, or Protestant. This leaves 3.4 billion who are still non-Christians, the largest groups being Hindus, Buddhists, and Muslims, most of whom live in the teeming continent of Asia. Like Goliath in David's day, these resistant peoples continue to "defy the armies of the living God."

Roman Catholic missionaries have been working in Asia for five hundred years and Protestant missionaries have been there for almost two hundred years. Yet only 3 percent of the people are Christians. This leaves 97 percent still to be won to faith in Christ. It is a sobering fact that there are more non-Christians in India and China than there are Christians in the entire world! It is unrealistic to suggest that the churches in Asia can finish the task without any help from the churches in the West. Korea obviously is an exception. With Christians now accounting for almost 25 percent of the population, the churches there may well be able to complete the evangelization of South Korea. But what about North Korea? If that country ever becomes free, the persecuted Christians, greatly reduced in numbers, will need massive aid from the outside.

In Black Africa we have done much better. There, almost 50 percent of the population are professing Christians; but the churches are in desperate need of Bible teaching. Converts are flocking into the church in such large numbers that it is impossible to adequately train them for church membership. Consequently many of these converts are bringing some of their paganism with them into the church. One recent study indicates that in Zaire 80 percent of the church members, when confronted with sickness or death, resort to animistic practices.

Latin America, of course, is claimed by the Roman Catholic Church, but the degree of nominalism is so high that Protestant mission boards have regarded Latin America as a bona fide mission field. The numbers of Evangelicals there are growing at an annual rate of 10 percent. In some countries, such as Guatemala, the growth rate is considerably higher. However, that growth is largely at the expense of the Roman Catholic Church. Consequently the ratio of Christians to non-Christians in that part of the world is not greatly affected.

What about the Muslim world, with 850 million people who are adamantly opposed to the gospel of Christ? Apart from Indonesia, the Muslim world has yielded few converts to the Christian faith, due largely to the Law of Apostasy that permits the local community to kill anyone who defects from the faith. For 1,300 years Islam has stood like an impregnable fortress. According to Patrick J. Johnstone, in *Operation World,* in the whole of the Middle East, after 160 years of missionary work, there are not more than five thousand converts from Islam. Obviously the unfinished task is enormous. Can we expect the largely stagnant churches in the Middle East to complete the evangelization of the Muslim world without outside help?

We are hearing a great deal these days about the "Hidden Peoples" of the world. According to Ralph D. Winter, director of the U.S. Center for World Mission, there are an estimated 17,000 of these hidden groups found in all parts of the world. These are cultural, social, economic, or linguistic groups in whose community there is no indigenous Christian movement. If they are to be reached at all, it must be by means of cross-cultural missions from outside. The watchword of this frontier movement is "A church for every people by the year 2000." The idea is a good one, but it is by no means certain that we will be able to achieve this goal in 15 short years.

There is one region of the world where we are actually losing ground—Europe. Once the locale of the Holy Roman Empire and the home of the Pietist Movement and the Protestant Reformation, Europe is fast becoming de-

Christianized. Hans Lilje, former bishop of the German Evangelical Church, stated, "The era when Europe was a Christian continent lies behind us." Speaking of Europe, Kenneth Scott Latourette stated, "Christians are tending to become minorities . . . the trend is toward de-Christianization of a predominantly Christian population." Once a great sending area, Europe is today a receiving area. Even with more than three thousand North American missionaries there, the churches in Europe have yet to be revived. Indeed, the most virile churches on the Continent are behind the Iron Curtain.

2. *Evangelism is a perennial task.* World evangelization is not something that can be achieved once and for all. Every generation needs to be evangelized all over again. Someone has said, "God has only children, no grandchildren." That is true. Every 30 years we have a new generation that needs to hear the gospel all over again. First-generation Christians are usually practicing Christians. The second generation is frequently much weaker, and the third generation, often weaker still. Stephen Neill laments that "the work in Dornakal [India] was very far from perfect. As we have already seen, at the end of his life, Bishop Azariah was distressed to find in the second and third generations of Christians less zeal and devotion than he had hoped for."[3] This is especially true in India and Indonesia where some of the churches are several hundred years old. There are, of course, obvious reasons for this sad state of affairs. After the second or third generation, Christianity tends to take on cultural overtones, and soon its members begin to take their heritage for granted and lose all desire to share their faith with their friends and neighbors. The churches turn inward on themselves, and soon their chief preoccupation is their own survival, not the salvation of the world.

---

3. Stephen Neill, *The Unfinished Task* (London: Edinburgh House, 1957), p. 129.

> In thinking about the church it is easy to slip into the erroneous idea that, because a country or parish has once been Christian it will remain so until the end of time. . . . One generation succeeds another, and that which comes is not naturally or inevitably Christian. . . . The task of the Church must always be unfinished, because so much energy must go into the endless business of winning the younger generation.[4]

That warning applies not only to other parts of the world. It applies to us as well. Here in the Western world some say we are living in a post-Christian era and no one can predict with any degree of certainty what the future holds. In the twenty-first century we may be receiving missionaries from Africa and Asia. Certainly secularization is rampant in the Western world, and unless we have a major revival such as England experienced under John Wesley, we may find our candlestick removed.

In spite of the fact that church membership in the United States remains high, Christian influence seems to be on the wane. According to the *U.S. News and World Report,* May 14, 1984, the church now ranks twenty-sixth in a list of 30 institutions that have an impact on "decisions affecting the nation as a whole." Consequently I am not very optimistic with regard to the future of Western civilization. It has probably seen its best days. Fifty years from now the balance of world power—political and economic—may be located in the Western Pacific. If China ever lines up with Japan, Korea, and Taiwan, we might easily see a major shift in the balance of world power.

3. *Evangelism is an attainable goal.* The end of all missionary endeavor is to win the world to Christ. That is implicit in His last command to go into all the world and make disciples of all nations. It is unthinkable that Jesus would have given His followers an impossible task. On the other hand, He made no attempt to conceal the problems involved in the operation. He clearly warned them of the

---

4. Ibid., p. 35.

difficulties and the dangers that lay ahead. He knew that, left to their own resources, they would never be able to fulfill the Great Commission. So, He promised them His own presence and the power of the Holy Spirit. He Himself would be with them, working in them, with them, and through them. Working together, they *could* win the world.

To talk this way is to expose oneself to the charge of "triumphalism." My reply is that there are two kinds of triumphalism—human and divine. If our triumphalism is born of human initiative, subject to human direction, and dependent on human endeavor, it is bad and should by all means be renounced. However, a study of the New Testament leads one to believe that the Great Commission was Christ's idea, not ours. It was to be undertaken at *His* command, supported by *His* power, and directed by *His* Spirit, for the honor of *His* name, for the praise of *His* glory, and for the ultimate achievement of *His* purpose. If that is triumphalism, so be it. It is His triumphalism, not ours. If, as we believe, He is the Head of the church and the Lord of history, then surely He has the right to speak and act in "triumphal" terms. That is His prerogative.

Having said this, we must go on to confess that the church, by her disobedience through the ages, has not measured up to her Lord's expectations. During long periods of time she turned inward and was completely preoccupied with her own internal problems and forgot her obligation to share the gospel with the world. As a result, except for the Syrian churches in South India, the Christian church throughout much of history was confined pretty much to the continent of Europe. It is only in the last two centuries that the Protestant churches have shown any interest in the world mission. And it has been a battle all along the way. To this day we are giving only a tiny part of our resources to the evangelization of the world.

It is estimated that 90 percent of all full-time Christian

workers are located in the West, which leaves only 10 percent for the three billion people in the rest of the world who are still without an adequate understanding of the gospel. Indeed, most of them have never seen a Bible, never met a single Christian, never heard the name of Christ—even as a swear word.

Now, for the first time in history we have the resources—personnel, funds, and facilities—to complete the task. The only question is: Do we have the will? Without that, we are not likely to complete the task of world evangelization in *any* generation. But the goal *is* attainable—if we are willing to put forth the required effort.

6

What I Believe about World Missions

The world mission of the Christian church has been around for a long time and through the years it has had its full share of supporters and detractors. During the late 1960s and the early 1970s the detractors were particularly vocal. Indeed, there were those who informed us that the missionary era was over. Books with such provocative titles as *Missionary, Go Home!*, *Missions in Crisis*, and *The End of an Era* came tumbling from the printing presses and countless articles along the same lines appeared in Christian periodicals. African leaders were calling for a five-year moratorium on Western missionaries and money. One African leader, referring to the missionaries, asked: "Why should someone save his soul at the expense of emasculating my humanity? Why should I be portrayed as a perpetually helpless nobody in order to reinforce the racial and spiritual arrogance of people in Europe and America?"[1] An Asian leader spoke of the death of the present missionary system and went on to say: "The most *missionary* service a missionary under the present system can do today in Asia is to go home."[2]

---

1. Burgess Carr, "Internationalizing the Mission," mimeographed paper, p. 4.
2. Emerito P. Nacpil, "Mission and Church in Asia but not Missionaries," p. 4.

And the critics were not all in foreign countries. We had critics at home as well. Indeed, some of them consider the entire missionary movement a mistake. One historian wrote, "There was something fundamentally unhealthy and incongruous in the whole missionary idea. . . . Only men of inner limitation, both intellectually, and spiritually, can gratuitously thrust their beliefs on others on the assumption that they alone have the truth."[3]

Having acquainted myself with various viewpoints on both sides of the question, and having myself been a participant in, and been a student of, missions for half a century, I offer my considered opinion on the missionary movement of the last two centuries.

A Magnificent Enterprise

The Christian mission is the most magnanimous, most magnificent enterprise the world has ever seen.

Some of us are old enough to remember the details of the Battle of Britain in the summer of 1940 when Adolf Hitler hurled the German air force at Britain, hoping in one knockout blow to bring the United Kingdom to its knees. The Royal Air Force, hopelessly outnumbered by the Germans, met the incoming planes and blasted them from the skies over England, thereby winning the Battle of Britain.

When it was all over, Prime Minister Winston Churchill paid tribute in the House of Commons to the brave men of the RAF in these words: "Never in the field of human conflict was so much owed by so many to so few." What Churchill said about the RAF may be said with equal truthfulness about the modern missionary movement. Never in the history of human endeavor have so many owed so much to so few. Tens of millions of people in all parts of the world are what they are today as a result,

---

3. Nathaniel Peffer, *The Far East: A Modern History* (Ann Arbor, Mich.: University of Michigan Press, 1958).

directly or indirectly, of the labors of a comparatively
small band of dedicated men and women known as missionaries.

Most of the leaders in Black Africa, whether in politics,
business, or the professions, received at least part of their
education in a mission school. Indeed, it is doubtful if
many countries in Black Africa would be independent today had it not been for the groundwork laid by the missionaries of an earlier day. When the missionaries arrived
in the nineteenth century only a handful of languages had
a written form. Today, more than six hundred languages
and dialects have been reduced to writing—all the work of
missionaries.

The impact of the gospel in Asia was not as dramatic as
in Africa; nevertheless, even there, it was the missionaries
who introduced modern medicine and Western education,
and thereby made a significant contribution to the mod-
ernization of large parts of Asia. Most reform movements
in China and India owed their inspiration, directly or indirectly, to Christianity. John Fairbank of Harvard has suggested that even the Communists in China borrowed a few
ideas from the missionaries.

During the nineteenth century three groups of Europeans were part of the outward thrust of the West into the
East—the diplomats, the merchants, and the missionaries. The first two went to get, not to give; and they were
not always very scrupulous about the means they em-
ployed. The missionaries were the only ones who went to
give and not to get. They gave all they had—time,
strength, money, love, and even life itself. In sickness and
in health, in peace and in war, in adversity and in prosperity, in life and in death, the missionaries were always
there—loving, caring, helping, healing, sharing.

By all odds the early missionaries were a special breed
of men and women. Single-handedly, and with great courage, they attacked the social evils of their time—child
marriage, the immolation of widows, temple prostitution,
and "untouchability" in India; the opium trade, gambling,

footbinding, and infanticide in China; the slave trade, polygamy, and the destruction of twins in Africa. In all parts of the world they opened schools, hospitals, medical colleges, clinics, orphanages, and leprosaria. They gave succor and sustenance to the dregs of society cast off by their own people. At great risk to themselves and their families they fought famines, floods, pestilence, and plagues. They were the first to rescue abandoned babies, educate girls, and liberate women. They reduced languages to writing, translated the Scriptures, and taught people to read, thereby opening to them a whole new world of ideas.

In the conduct of their work they encountered indifference, suspicion, hostility, persecution, and imprisonment. Times without number their homes were looted, their buildings burned, their churches desecrated, and their lives threatened. Thousands returned home broken in health. Other thousands died prematurely of tropical diseases. Hundreds became martyrs. And all this they endured without reserve, without regret, and without reward.

This is not to whitewash the missionaries. They were not angels; they were not even saints. But they were, in the words of Pearl S. Buck, "born warriors and very great men." They had their full share of idiosyncrasies. They had their headaches and their hang-ups. They had their doubts and their fears. Touch them, and they were touchy. Cross them and they got cross. There were limits to their endurance. They cracked up physically, mentally, morally, and spiritually. They have been known to fall into sin, including adultery, homosexuality, and suicide. Not all missionaries have been happily married. Not all missionaries' children have turned out well. Some have gone astray. Some resented the fact that their parents were missionaries. A few ended up as agnostics and alcoholics.

Is it possible to make a balanced judgment of such people? Kenneth Scott Latourette has probably come closer to the truth than anyone else. What he said about missionaries in China can be applied to missionaries in general.

The missionaries were the one group of foreigners whose major endeavor was to make the impact of the West upon the Middle Kingdom of benefit to the Chinese. Bigoted and narrow they frequently were, occasionally superstitious, and sometimes domineering and serenely convinced of the superiority of Western culture and of their own particular form of Christianity. When all that can be said in criticism of the missionaries has been said, however, and it is not a little, the fact remains that nearly always at considerable and very often at great sacrifice they came to China, and in unsanitary and uncongenial surroundings, usually with insufficient stipends, often at the cost of their own lives, or the lives that were dearer to them than their own, labored indefatigably for an alien people who did not want them or their message. Whatever may be the final judgment on the major premises, the methods, and the results of the missionary enterprise, the fact cannot be gainsaid that for sheer altruism and heroic faith here is one of the bright pages in the history of the race.[4]

The Prime Function of the Christian Church

The church has at least five functions: worship, teaching, fellowship, service, and missions or witness. Which of these is the *prime* function of the church in the world between Pentecost and the Second Advent? If the Acts of the Apostles and the practice of the early church are anything to go by, we would have to select witness. The other four functions will be continued in heaven, presumably in higher, purer form. Only one—witness—will not survive the Rapture. That in itself puts witness in a class by itself. The church is to extend her witness to the ends of the earth (Acts 1:8) and to the end of time (Mt 28:20).

The church, as described by Luke in the Book of Acts, is preeminently a witnessing community—and this because

---

4. Kenneth Scott Latourette, *A History of Christian Missions in China* (New York: Macmillan, 1929), pp. 824–25.

of the nature conferred on her by the Holy Spirit at Pentecost. In Acts 1:8 we read: "You shall be my witnesses both in Jerusalem, and in all Judea and Samaria, and even to the remotest part of the earth." In Acts 2:4 we read: "And they were all filled with the Holy Spirit and began to speak with other tongues, as the Spirit was giving them utterance."

It is obvious from these two passages that the validity of the world mission is rooted in the nature of the church. What, we may ask, is the essential nature of the church? What kind of community did God intend the church to be? Harry R. Boer has this to say:

> The Great Commission derives its meaning and power wholly and exclusively from the Pentecost event. It does so in terms of a deeply organic relationship. . . . The proclamation of the gospel is therefore not one activity among many in which the Church of the New Testament engages; but it is her basic, her essential activity. It is for this reason that the preaching office is the central office in the Church.[5]

When Emil Brunner said that the church exists by mission as fire exists by burning, he expressed a profound truth. Lesslie Newbigin said that a church that has lost its missionary vision no longer has the right to be called a New Testament church. Such a church has denied the faith and betrayed its trust.

Luke tells us that when the early disciples were filled with the Holy Spirit at Pentecost they began to speak with other tongues. It is a great pity that Bible expositors have made such an issue of the "tongues" and thereby missed the real point of the passage. They were all filled with the Holy Spirit and began to speak . . . and they kept on speaking, speaking, speaking, until they were accused in

---

5. Harry R. Boer, *Pentecost and Missions* (Grand Rapids: Eerdmans, 1961), p. 119.

almost no time at all of filling Jerusalem with the doctrine (Acts 5:28).

The kind of witnessing we see in the early church was natural, spontaneous, joyous, and compulsive. Why? Because it was the natural, inevitable expression of the nature the church was given at Pentecost. Boer goes on to say:

> When a given activity is not accidental to the life of an organism, but an essential manifestation of it, that activity may be said to be an expression of the organism's being. It is an expression of its deepest nature. It is in this way that we must regard the witnessing activity of the Church. The kerygmatic activity of the Church is an expression of the law that governs the discharge of her task in the world. This law is the Great Commission. At Pentecost this law went into effect. The Great Commission is the mandate to witness universally. . . . At Pentecost the Church became a witnessing institute because the coming of the Spirit made Christ's mandate an organic part of her being, an essential expression of her life.[6]

It is difficult to read the Acts of the Apostles carefully and escape the conviction that the principal activity of the church in the apostolic age was witnessing. It stands out clearly in almost every chapter.

This is especially true when we examine the ministry of the apostles. So powerful, and successful, was their witness that it provoked reaction on the part of the Sanhedrin. Peter and John were called before the council and commanded not to speak any more in the name of Jesus. Their reply was significant: "We cannot stop speaking what we have seen and heard" (Acts 4:20). Note the word *cannot*. It was not an act of defiance. It was a matter of compulsion. They couldn't help themselves. For when the council forbade the apostles to witness they were asking them to violate a basic law of their nature. Hence their reply: "We *cannot* stop speaking."

---

6. Ibid., pp. 119–20.

Even when persecution broke out and the disciples were scattered all over the eastern end of the Mediterranean world, everywhere they went they took the gospel with them. Luke says that they went everywhere "preaching the word" (Acts 8:4).

After being released by the council the apostles prayed not for safety but for courage to *speak* the Word. Their prayer was answered, they were again filled with the Holy Spirit, and they continued to *speak* the Word of God with boldness (Acts 4:31). After the seven deacons were chosen, the Word of God kept on spreading (Acts 6:7). And the opponents in the synagogues were unable to resist the wisdom and the spirit with which Stephen spoke (Acts 6:10). It was impossible to silence or suppress the apostles. Forbid them to speak and they go right on speaking. Put them in jail and at midnight they sing praises. Release them from prison and the next day they are back in the temple, teaching. At the end of his ministry, Paul, the greatest of all the apostles, could say, "Having obtained help from God, I stand to this day testifying both to small and great" (Acts 26:22).

The Most Difficult of Christian Vocations

World missions is the most difficult of all Christian vocations. Stephen Neill in *Call to Mission* has said, "Christian missionary work is the most difficult thing in the world. It is surprising that it should ever have been attempted." Most missionaries will agree with Neill. Missionary work *is* difficult. It is difficult primarily because of the opposition it encounters.

When one stops to think of it, the Great Commission as given by Christ was an astounding proposition. Eleven men were saddled with the responsibility of winning the world for Christ. The very idea must have seemed preposterous to the twelve apostles, already reduced to eleven by the death of Judas.

The task was formidable. Their chances of success were almost nil. They had no central organization, no financial resources, few influential friends, and no political machine. Certainly they had no army.

Arrayed against them was the ecclesiastical power of the Sanhedrin, the political power and military might of Rome, and the religious fanaticism of the Jews. Little wonder that Jesus warned them to remain in Jerusalem until they were endued with power from on high.

In New Testament times and throughout history opposition to Christian missions has come from four sources. We shall discuss each one very briefly.

Religious Fanaticism

The Jews of Jesus' day are a classic example of this kind of opposition. There is a well-meaning attempt today to exonerate the Jews for the death of Christ. It is a fact that the persecution that raged around the person of Christ, and ultimately doomed Him to the death of the cross, came from His own people, especially the leaders. All the major parties—Pharisees, Sadducees, Herodians, and Scribes—did their best to destroy Him, and finally succeeded.

Their opposition seemed to stem from blind fanaticism and there is no fanaticism quite as dangerous as religious fanaticism. And why did they oppose Him? They opposed Him because He was too good for them. They hated Him, as Jesus said, "without a cause" (Jn 15:25). The beauty of His holiness was in stark contrast to their self-righteous behavior based on law but devoid of love. And the fact that the common people heard Him gladly served only to deepen and darken their hatred, until they could stand Him no longer, and they arranged to have Him crucified.

And Jesus warned His disciples that they would encounter the same kind of opposition from the same source. "They will make you outcasts from the synagogue," He said, "but an hour is coming for everyone who kills you to think that he is offering service to God" (Jn 16:2).

These words were literally fulfilled in the life of Saul of Tarsus. By his own confession, he entered every one of the four hundred synagogues in Jerusalem, apprehended all the Christians he could round up, and committed them to prison. And when they were condemned to death he cast his vote against them.

Later on, following his conversion, Saul got a taste of his own medicine. For the remainder of his life he was never free from persecution at the hands of his own people for whose salvation he longed and labored. Finally they turned him over to the Romans and he was executed by them in the city of Rome.

In our own day the Christian mission encounters similar opposition, especially in Asia. We have done exceedingly well in Africa, the homeland of animism, but Asia has been a different story. There the missionary encountered the great, powerful religious structures of Hinduism, Buddhism, and Islam, not to mention Confucianism. The average American church member has no idea of how extremely difficult it is to make converts in Asia. After five hundred years of missionary effort only 3 percent of the population have embraced the Christian faith.

These ancient religions have their own founders, philosophers, teachers, and reformers. They have beautiful temples, stupas, pagodas, and monasteries. They have their holy men: fakirs, swamis, yogis, and gurus. They also have their sacred scriptures and their gods and goddesses by the millions. They even have their own saviors and their *bodhisattvas*.

Before a Buddhist or a Brahmin can be converted he must be persuaded that Christianity is true; and if Christianity is true, his religion is false—not *totally* false, but basically false. If the Christian doctrine of God is true, then the Hindu doctrine of God must be false. No one likes to be told, especially by an outsider, that his religion is false.

How is the Buddhist going to be persuaded to give up his

books and beads when his forefathers used them from time immemorial? How can the missionary persuade the Brahmin to break caste or the Confucianist to give up ancestor worship?

And if it is difficult to convert a Buddhist or a Hindu, what about a Muslim? He knows just enough about Christianity to inoculate him against the real thing. He has a high regard for Jesus as the Son of Mary, but adamantly rejects both the deity and the death of Christ. For 1,300 years he and his forefathers have been taught that it is not only heresy but also blasphemy to suggest that God could have a son.

In Islam the Law of Apostasy permits the community to kill a defector from the faith. Needless to say, that is a strong deterrent to anyone considering accepting the Christian faith. Such an act requires superhuman courage. A veteran missionary to the Middle East had this to say: "So confined is the Muslim that in some countries of the Middle East a follower of Islam who changed his religion would in effect be tearing up his birth certificate, citizenship papers, voting registration, and work permit; and would become a man without a country."[7] Making converts in Asia has been exceedingly difficult.

Racial Prejudice

In our day racial prejudice is generally regarded as the monopoly of the white race. Admittedly our guilt in this respect is very great, but racial prejudice has been around for a long time. It is found in all parts of the world. The French regard themselves as the guardians of European civilization. Consequently they look down on the Ger-

---

7. R. Park Johnson, *Middle East Pilgrimage* (New York: Friendship, 1958), p. 142.

mans. The Germans, in turn, look down on the English.
And all three look down on us Americans! In Asia the
paramount groups despise, and often exploit, the ab-
origines.

Along with racial prejudice goes cultural pride. Paul
encountered this problem when he addressed the philosophers in Athens. His message was cogent, conciliatory,
and captivating. It was designed to disarm their prejudice,
satisfy their curiosity, and impart to them the truth
concerning God's activity in creation, redemption, and
judgment. It was a brilliant address, punctuated with ref-
erences to their poets and couched in philosophical terms
likely to appeal to their intellectual interests. They listened intently until he mentioned the Resurrection; at
that point they laughed him to scorn.

Missionaries in Asia have encountered the same kind of
prejudice based on culture. The Brahmins in India have
alway been very proud of their social status, and would
have nothing to do with the low-caste Sudras. Imagine
how they felt when they discovered that Jesus was a carpenter and His disciples were mostly fishermen—both
groups being a subcaste of the Sudra caste in India.

The situation was much the same in China, known as
the Middle Kingdom. For well over a thousand years
China shed the light and luster of her superior civilization
over a large part of Asia. She lent to everyone; she borrowed from no one. As far as the Chinese were concerned
there was only one civilized country—the Middle Kingdom. All others were beyond the pale and regarded as
"barbarians."

Everywhere the missionaries went they were opposed
by the scholar/gentry class, who regarded them as a threat
to their position and prestige as the undisputed leaders in
society. With every weapon at their command they tried to
discredit Christianity. They even went so far as to declare,
"We would sooner go to hell with our Confucius than go to
heaven with your Jesus." Little wonder that Christian
missionaries won so few converts in China—never more
than 1 percent of the population.

National Chauvinism

The Roman Empire was one of the great empires of history and its citizens were naturally proud of their empire with all its pomp, pageantry, and power; so much so that they regarded the Jews as the "second race" and the Christians as the "third race" in the empire.

On several occasions nationalism proved inimical to the progress of the gospel. On two occasions Paul and his gospel were rejected because he and his message were Jewish. In the Roman colony of Philippi Paul and Silas ended up in prison. The accusation made against them was, "These men are throwing our city into confusion, being Jews, and are proclaiming customs which it is not lawful for us to accept or to observe, being Romans" (Acts 16:20–21).

Whether Paul's doctrine was good or bad, true or false, was beside the point. It was *foreign,* and therefore unacceptable. In Thessalonica they were accused of acting "contrary to the decrees of Caesar, saying that there is another king, Jesus" (Acts 17:7).

Nationalism is without doubt one of the greatest problems facing the missionary today. With the collapse of the vast colonial system, nationalism has taken over and walls are being erected in all parts of the world. Some countries have closed their doors to Christian missionaries. Indigenous cultures are being revived and refurbished, and Christians are viewed with suspicion if they fail to participate in various aspects of the renaissance.

Almost everywhere Christianity is regarded as a Western import. In Asia it is called a "foreign religion." In Africa it is known as the "white man's religion." This makes life very difficult for Christian converts who are vulnerable at this point. They want to be good Christians and loyal citizens at the same time, but the odds are against them. Often they are treated as second-class citizens. This is especially true in countries with a state religion. In Thailand, for instance, to be a good Thai is to be a

Buddhist. To be a Christian, even a patriotic one, is to be a second-class citizen.

Economic Interests

Charles Wilson, one-time president of General Motors, said on one occasion, "What's good for General Motors is good for the United States." To this day, some people have not forgiven him for that statement. Calvin Coolidge said, "The business of America is business." Both men have been reviled for their brash statements. The fact is that both men spoke the truth.

One does not have to fully agree with Karl Marx's doctrine of economic determinism, but surely there is an element of truth in what he said. The bottom line is profit—every time. Men and nations will do for money what they won't do for anything else. Communist China's present rapprochement with the United States, the great bastion of capitalism, is economically inspired. Touch a person's pocketbook and you have touched the apple of his eye.

On at least two occasions the apostle Paul ran afoul of business interests, once in Philippi and again in Ephesus. In Philippi a demon-possessed young woman brought her masters much profit by fortunetelling. When the demon was exorcised, the woman was of no further use to her masters. And Luke adds, "When her masters saw that their hope of profit was gone, they seized Paul and Silas and dragged them into the market place before the authorities" (Acts 16:19). As a result, the two apostles were beaten and thrown into prison.

A similar situation developed in Ephesus, the center of the worship of the goddess Artemis. The response to the gospel was such that a large number of people abandoned the worship of Artemis. The silversmiths, who made and sold small images of Artemis, found their business dropping off drastically, at which point they called for a protest meeting addressed by Demetrius. Said he:

Men, you know that our prosperity depends upon this business. And you see and hear that not only in Ephesus, but in almost all of Asia, this Paul has persuaded and turned away a considerable number of people, saying that gods made with hands are no gods at all. And not only is there danger that this trade of ours fall into disrepute, but also that the temple of the great goddess Artemis be regarded as worthless. . . . [Acts 19:25–27]

In the modern missionary enterprise the same conflict can be seen. The merchants and the missionaries were the two groups involved in the heyday of colonialism. They came from the same countries. They traveled on the same ships. They lived and labored under the protection of the same flag.

In the seventeenth and eighteenth centuries the great East India Companies had a virtual monopoly on ocean travel and world trade. Missionaries were at the mercy of these powerful mercantile firms. Often they were denied passage on their ships. In some countries they were not permitted to live or work in their domain. The British East India Company certainly had no love for the missionaries. Its directors stated their view quite plainly: "The sending out of missionaries into our Eastern possessions is the maddest, most extravagant, most costly, most indefensible project which has ever been suggested by a moonstruck fanatic. It strikes against all reason and sound policy. It brings the peace and safety of our possessions into peril."

The two groups were poles apart in their philosophy. The merchants went to the East to buy and sell and make a handsome profit, and they were not always honest in their dealings. The missionaries, on the other hand, went to the East to help, to heal, to build.

Then, as now, there was considerable exploitation on the part of the businessmen. The missionaries, by their very presence, if not by their protest, were a thorn in the side of the exploiters. Whether it was the opium trade in China, the slave trade in East Africa, the liquor traffic in West Africa, or the shameful exploitation of indentured labor in the South Pacific, the missionaries were the only ones to raise a protest, and in so doing they made more enemies than friends.

The situation has improved greatly in the twentieth century, but exploitation has by no means been eliminated. The huge and powerful multinational corporations represent a new form of economic exploitation. On the surface they appear to be more humane, but in fact they demand their last pound of flesh.

Certainly the "dollar diplomacy" practiced by Uncle Sam in Latin America in the first half of this century did nothing to enhance the image of the American missionary. He too is a *gringo*.

The Possibility of Persecution

World missions may be entering a period of persecution. Up to now, we have had it so good that it seems strange to talk about persecution. During the nineteenth century the colonial system, for all its faults, provided the Christian missionary with almost universal protection. China, which never became a colony of any one power, was an exception. There the Christian mission suffered heavy casualties. In 1900, 189 Protestant missionaries and their children were killed by the Boxers. But in other parts of Asia and throughout the whole of Africa Christian missionaries lived and labored under the protection of some European flag. Now that the colonial system is dead, the situation has changed, and in the future we may see the casualty rate climb.

Persecution should not surprise us. When Jesus sent out the Twelve (Mt 10), He took pains to warn them of the kind of opposition they were likely to encounter. He pulled no punches. He told them frankly what kind of treatment they could expect at the hands of a cruel, hostile world. Indeed, His statement of the Great Commission in Matthew 28 was tantamount to a declaration of war against the demonic forces of the world. Jesus laid down certain principles which are as valid today as they were then.

The Inevitability of Conflict

Jesus said, "Do not think that I came to bring peace on the earth; I did not come to bring peace, but a sword" (Mt 10:34). Again He said, "In the world you have tribulation" (Jn 16:33). Truth unites but it also divides. It unites all who accept it. It divides all who reject it.

The apostle Paul's ministry was confined mostly to the Jewish synagogues where he expected to find an intelligent, sympathetic audience. But in every synagogue he succeeded in dividing the congregation into two opposing sides. There were those who followed him and those who fought him.

The Likelihood of Personal Danger

"Beware of men," Jesus said, "for they will deliver you up to the courts, and scourge you in their synagogues" (Mt 10:17). He went on to say, "An hour is coming for everyone who kills you to think that he is offering service to God" (Jn 16:2).

This is precisely what happened in the early church. There was hardly a city in which Paul's ministry did not terminate abruptly in a citywide riot that almost cost him his life. Damascus, Jerusalem, Antioch, Iconium, Lystra, Derbe, Philippi, Thessalonica, Berea, Corinth, Ephesus—in all of them Paul found that "bonds and afflictions" awaited him. Jesus warned them that preaching could be a hazardous occupation. It was for Stephen, James, Paul, and a host of others.

The Need to Persevere

Again, the words of Jesus come through loud and clear: "Do not fear those who kill the body, but are unable to kill

the soul. . . . Whenever they persecute you in this city, flee
to the next. . . . He who has found his life shall lose it, and
he who has lost his life for My sake shall find it" (Mt 10:28,
23, 39).

The twelve apostles learned their lesson well. They suffered persecution without retaliating, asking only for
courage to endure (Acts 4:29). They joyfully took the spoil-
ing of their goods (Heb 10:34), knowing that their real
treasure was in heaven (Mt 6:10). They faced beatings and
imprisonment with a cheerfulness that left their per-
secutors completely nonplussed (Acts 4:16). They refused
to be intimidated even by death (Acts 21:13). And those
who were called on to seal their testimony with their blood
asked only that their enemies might be forgiven (Acts
7:60).

Such was the missionary zeal of those first-century
Christians. With no weapon but truth and no banner but
love they pressed on day after day, teaching and preaching
the most revolutionary message the Roman world had
ever heard, until the mighty empire cracked wide open
and the emperor bowed the knee to Jesus Christ.

Who knows what the future holds for the Christian mission? We may be in for some difficult days. We should not
assume that the Christian missionary will continue to
receive the preferential treatment he has enjoyed in the
past. We are living in a new day—the postcolonial era—
and we must expect major changes in the situation in the
Third World. The overthrow of the Shah of Iran and the
seizure of power by Ayatollah Ruhollah Khomeini in 1979
has introduced a new element into the already volatile
situation in the Middle East. The war between Iran and
Iraq still hangs in the balance; should Iran win the war,
Islamic fundamentalism is likely to spill over into the Gulf
States. With the active cooperation of Khomeini and Colo-
nel Muammar Qadhafi of Libya, Islam is on the march and
woe betide anyone who gets in the way. Even the gentle,
peaceful members of the Bahai faith in Iran are being

systematically eliminated and President Ronald Reagan was the only world leader to raise a protest.

All around the world religious freedom is eroding under dictatorships of the right and the left. Hindu extremists in India are calling for the expulsion of all missionaries from that country and the suppression of all other religions. In the Hindu kingdom of Nepal the constitution forbids anyone from changing his or her religion. Those accepting Christian baptism are subject to imprisonment. Among those in prison are some pastors and evangelists. The tentmaking missionaries with the United Mission to Nepal are required to refrain from all attempts to "proselytize." The same is true of a handful of tentmakers in Afghanistan.

Ever since a Marxist regime came to power in Ethiopia in 1974 the Christian churches have been under varying degrees of pressure and persecution.

During the last five years hundreds of Protestant churches in isolated provinces have been closed, some of which were later permitted to reopen. Today nearly 1,800 of the Word of Life's 2,500 churches are closed. At various times during the last couple of years as many as 20 church leaders have been in prison at the same time.

The second largest denomination (700,000), the Mekane Yesus Church, affiliated with the Lutheran World Federation, is suffering the same fate. About one-quarter of its two thousand churches are closed. Hundreds of church leaders and members have been in prison for varying periods of time during the last five years. The much smaller Meserete Kristos Church (Mennonite) has been hardest hit of all. All its churches have been disbanded and most of its top leaders have been in prison for years.

Of course, Ethiopia is not the only Communist country in which the Christian church is fighting with its back to the wall. In some countries, such as North Korea, the organized church has disappeared. In other countries, such as Vietnam, China, the Soviet Union, and the Eastern European countries, the churches are permitted to worship but not witness, to exist but not expand.

Several pastors in Mindanao have been killed by Moro insurgents demanding autonomy from the central government in Manila. Ninety evangelical pastors in Peru have been cruelly murdered by the Marxist insurgents trying to overthrow the government. Just last year 21 churches in Northern Nigeria were burned down by fanatical Muslims, and to date authorities have refused permission to rebuild. In Northeast India Christians have been attacked and churches burned by Hindu extremists. In Egypt the Coptic Church, which goes back to the first century, is under attack. Its head, Pope Shenouda III, spent several years in exile in a monastery in Sinai. A recent report by the American Coptic Association cites a number of cases of government-inspired persecution, such as the seizure of church trust lands, hospitals, and schools. No Christian can hold any one of the top 160 appointive positions in or out of politics.

The fate of Lebanon still hangs in the balance, but if the Muslims can seize power and change the constitution, the Christians, who once represented slightly more than half of the population, may find themselves not only out of power but also out of favor. One radical group, known as *Jihad* (Holy War), has threatened to kill all Americans in the Middle East if their demands are not met. At this writing, five Americans are being held for ransom; all we can do is wait, hope, and pray.

There are many countries that, though they stop short of persecution, are gradually closing their doors to missionaries. At the present time it is virtually impossible to get new missionaries into India, Pakistan, and Indonesia. Other countries, such as Bangladesh, Thailand, and Taiwan, are limiting the number of missionaries that may enter in any given year. Other countries, such as Nigeria, Venezuela, the Philippines, and Brazil, have from time to time indefinitely delayed the granting of visas. Others will grant a visa but withhold a work permit. In some countries it is necessary to get a work permit before teaching Sunday school.

In certain parts of Latin America the Roman Catholic Church is concerned about the rapid growth of the Evangelicals. On November 9, 1984, an apostolic delegate representing the Vatican in Mexico, Jeronomi Prigione, declared that Latin American governments should take action to "counteract the activity" and "nullify the influence" of Protestant groups. About the same time two influential newspapers in Mexico City called for the immediate expulsion of Wycliffe Bible Translators, ostensibly because they were undermining Latin American culture.

Is the missionary enterprise, based in the West, in danger of coming to an end? Some people have fears along this line. Peter Octavianus, one of the outstanding leaders in Indonesia, said, "Missionary work as such, done by expatriates, appears to be coming to an end in the days ahead."

If the casualty rate continues to increase will the church in America continue to support the missionary enterprise, or will it call for a withdrawal of our missionaries? The latter is what happened in Zaire in the early 1960s. After the Simbas went on the rampage and murdered almost two hundred missionaries, most of them Roman Catholics, an article in one leading evangelical magazine called for the withdrawal of all missionaries from Zaire. One thing seems certain: The American people will not tolerate heavy casualties unless our own survival is at stake. Events in Vietnam and, more recently, Lebanon confirm that point. Will the church follow the government and recall its missionaries when the going gets rough?

There is an alternative to pulling out. We might call for missionary volunteers, single men, who will be willing for a term of four or five years to serve, without any thought of marriage, in some of the more dangerous parts of the world. The Roman Catholic Church has always had religious orders made up of men and women who agree to remain single for life. Maybe the time has come to challenge some of our young people to remain single for a term or two. Certainly they would be more mobile, carry fewer burdens, and be more effective in some situations than married missionaries with wives and children to care for.

Mission's Continuity to the End of the Age

Other movements come and go, but the missionary movement will continue until the age ends with the Second Coming. And this we have on the authority of Christ Himself. In Matthew 24:14 He declared, "This gospel of the kingdom shall be preached in the whole world for a witness to all the nations, and then the end shall come." In the Great Commission in Matthew 28, Jesus promised to be with His witnesses to the end of the age.

The Peace Corps, launched by President John F. Kennedy in the early 1960s, was one of the finest things the United States ever did in the area of foreign aid. For a time, the Peace Corps was very popular. Applications were received at the rate of five thousand a month, and by 1968 there were 14,000 volunteers in some 60 countries. By 1970 the Peace Corps was beginning to lose some of its glamor, and today the budget has been slashed by Congress and the number of volunteers is only 5,200. Unless someone can give the Peace Corps a blood transfusion, by the end of the decade this noble experiment may come to an end.

In contrast, the modern missionary movement that got under way with William Carey in 1793 is about to celebrate its bicentennial. Year after year a steady stream of missionaries leaves our shores for overseas service; today there are more missionaries in more countries of the world than at any time in two thousand years of church history. In December 1984 more than 18,000 young people gave up their Christmas vacation to attend the famous Urbana Missionary Convention sponsored by Inter-Varsity Christian Fellowship.

When Jesus gave His disciples their marching orders, He did not paint a rosy picture. He told them quite honestly the conditions under which they would have to live and labor. The missionary enterprise would be fraught with all kinds of difficulties and dangers. The messengers of the cross would be hunted and hounded from pillar to post. They would be scourged in the Jewish synagogues and flogged by Roman officials, and some of them would die a martyr's death. But the mandate would never be rescinded nor the mission aborted.

Neither the mischief of men nor the machinations of the devil were to deter them. They were taught to believe that they were engaged in a holy war with an implacable foe who would not surrender without a life-and-death struggle (Eph 6:10–12; 1 Pet 5:8). Casualties would occur and reverses come, but they were to press on in full confidence that the Captain of their salvation would be with them to the end of the age. Many battles would be lost, but the war would be won. On that point there was no doubt (Rom 8:35–39; 2 Cor 2:14).

We do well to bear this in mind when the modern prophets of doom are sounding the death knell of the Christian mission. We are being told on every hand that the Christian mission is at the crossroads. Indeed? That's interesting! It has always been at the crossroads. That is where it began. That is where it belongs. That is where it will remain to the end of time.

Mao Zedong said on one occasion that a revolution is not a tea party. He ought to know, for he was without doubt the greatest revolutionary of the twentieth century, and fought his way, through 22 years of intermittent guerrilla warfare, to victory in 1949. He then presided over one-quarter of the human race for almost 30 years. Well, what Chairman Mao said about the revolution can be said with equal truthfulness about the world mission of the Christian church. It is not a tea party! It is spiritual warfare and in every war there are defeats, reverses, and casualties. But the *war* goes on!

Dictators come and go, kingdoms rise and fall, civilizations wax and wane, but the worldwide mission of the church will continue to the end of the age in spite of all the vicissitudes of world history. When one door closes, another will open. If Western missionaries are expelled, non-Westerners will take their place. If *all* missionaries are expelled from a given country, the indigenous church will still be there to carry on. If the indigenous church is forced to go underground, the Holy Spirit will remain to carry on His own work. It is one thing to get rid of the missionaries; it is quite another to remove God. Heaven is His throne and earth is His footstool. It is impossible to banish Him from any part of His domain.

There is plenty of evidence for this in recent history. When the missionaries were expelled from Ethiopia by Benito Mussolini in 1937 they left behind a handful of Christians. Eight years later, at the close of the war, 18,000 baptized believers greeted the returning missionaries! When the missionaries had to leave Mozambique in the late 1960s they left behind a small group of 3,600 baptized believers. When they returned in 1983 they found a church of 400,000! A similar thing happened in Angola, another Marxist country. It was closed to missionaries for almost 20 years. When the first Church of God missionary returned in 1983 he discovered to his delight that the number of believers had increased from 3,000 to 200,000!

Mention has already been made of the situation in Nepal. David M. Howard, general director of World Evangelical Fellowship, visited Nepal in January 1984 and reported that the number of Christians in that tiny country, in spite of government persecution, soared from 500 in 1979 to 15,000 in 1984. Howard states, "There is a sense of excitement there. They told me that in the 50s and 60s, when they were just getting started, the church seemed to have a survival complex; just hanging on, wanting only to survive. Now the church is getting very aggressive, and there is real revival in several areas."[8]

8. *Missionary News Service*, March 1, 1984, p. 3.

Of one thing we may be sure. The modern missionary movement is God's enterprise, not man's, and He is well able to take care of His own enterprise. The kingdom is His, the church is His, the power is His, and the glory is His. In spite of all evidence to the contrary, this world is God's world. He is in ultimate control, and He has no intention whatever of abdicating. The missionary movement of our time is part and parcel of His plan for the world, and it will continue to the end of the age.

PART 3

The Response
The World Christians We Must Be

7

The Marks of a World Christian

In Matthew 13 Jesus gives us a panoramic view of the development and expansion of the kingdom from Pentecost to the end of the age. In two of the seven parables—the first and the second—Jesus speaks of the seed or the "good seed." In the first parable the seed is equated with the *word* of the kingdom. In the other the "good seed" is said to be the *children* of the kingdom (vv. 24, 38). In our evangelistic preaching, we have paid much more attention to the first than to the second, but both are important.

The "word," of course, is the gospel. The "children" are those in whom the "word" has taken root and brought forth fruit. The kingdom, then, comes in two forms—verbal and vital. Both forms are to play an important role in the extension of the kingdom to the end of time and to the ends of the earth. The "word" of the kingdom falls into the soil of the human heart and there brings forth fruit unto eternal life. The "children" of the kingdom are those true believers who, in the course of time, will be scattered over the face of the earth, where they will settle down and form the nucleus of the kingdom of God in various kinds of cultural and religious "soil."

As a child of the kingdom the believer then becomes a World Christian. By calling he belongs to a universal fellowship—the Christian church. By conviction he proclaims a universal message—the Christian gospel. By commitment he owes his allegiance to a universal king—Jesus Christ. By vocation, he is a part of a universal movement—the Christian mission.

Not all believers, however, live up to their high calling as World Christians. The vast majority are just "ethnic" Christians—American, Canadian, Norwegian, or Chinese, as the case might be. Others are content to be "denominational" Christians, concerned only with the affairs of their own particular denomination.

What, we may ask, are some of the truths that a World Christian accepts?

The Universal Fatherhood of God

A World Christian is one who acknowledges the universal fatherhood of God. Some evangelicals reject the phrase *fatherhood of God* along with the concomitant phrase *brotherhood of man*. One reason for this is the fact that these two terms have been widely used by our liberal friends, and that, we sometimes think, makes them suspect. However, we must understand that the phrase *fatherhood of God* can be used in two ways—in relation to creation or in relation to redemption. If we are thinking of the latter, then we had better not use the term; for in that sense not all men are children of God. They are children of the devil. Jesus said so (Jn 8:44).

However, with respect to creation, the Bible clearly teaches that all mankind has come from one root, Adam, who was the "son of God" (Lk 3:38). The Bible opens with the majestic statement: "In the beginning God created the heavens and the earth" (Gen 1:1). That makes Him the creator, sustainer, and controller of the universe. The psalmist narrows it down and says, "The earth is the LORD's, and all it contains, the world and those who dwell in it" (Ps 24:1). That makes Him the King of the nations and the Father of the human race. All men belong to Him

by right of creation, whether or not they know it or acknowledge it. The prodigal son was his father's son even in
the far country, long before he decided to return home.
That is precisely why the father yearned for his return.
That parable is a powerful symbol of the universal fatherhood of God.

The brotherhood of man is also a thoroughly biblical
doctrine. Jesus, for instance, taught His disciples to pray,
"Our Father who art in heaven, hallowed be Thy name"
(Mt 6:9). If there is only one father in heaven, it stands to
reason there can be only one family on earth—the human
family. Anthropologists have a way of dividing mankind in
"races." At one time they spoke of seven races. Later they
reduced the number to three. Now, I understand, they are
back up presently to thirty-two! But whether the number
is seven, or three, or thirty-two makes no difference to
God. As far as He is concerned there is only one race—the
human race.

Paul made that abundantly clear in his address to the
philosophers in Athens. He declared, "The God who made
the world and all things in it . . . made from one, every
nation of mankind to live on all the face of the earth . . . for
in Him we live and move and exist, as even some of your
own poets have said, 'For we also are His offspring'" (Acts
17:24–28).

In another place Paul refers to God as the "Savior of all
men, especially of believers" (1 Tim 4:10). If that is true,
there is surely a sense in which God is the *Father* of all
men, especially of believers. In Ephesians 3:15 Paul
speaks of "every family in heaven and on earth" as deriv-
ing its name from God the Father. There is a sense, then, in
which God is the Father of the human family.

If this is so, then every man is my brother and every
woman is my sister, regardless of race, class, color, culture,
or any other human factor. I may live in affluent America
and he or she may live in poverty-stricken Bangladesh. It
makes no difference; we are children of the same father
(Eph 4:6) and members of the same family (Eph 3:15). We

have a common origin—Adam (1 Cor 15:45–49). We share a common problem—sin (Rom 5:12). We face a common destiny—death (Heb 9:27). These are fundamental, indisputable, unchanging facts that cannot be altered by such incidental factors as ethnic origin, social status, cultural mores, or linguistic differences.

The Universal Lordship of Christ

A World Christian is one who confesses the universal lordship of Christ. In our well-meaning but ill-advised manner of speaking we often talk about our "making Jesus Lord." No man, not even the Christian, can "make" Jesus Lord. That is something that God, the Father, did when He raised Jesus from the dead and set Him at His own right hand far above all principality and power and might and dominion (Eph 1:21–22), and gave Him a name that is above every name; that at the name of Jesus every knee should bow and that every tongue should confess that Jesus Christ is Lord (Ph 2:9–11).

Julius Caesar is always the Roman; Socrates is always the Greek. Confucius is always the Chinese. But Jesus Christ is not to be identified with any one race, people, or culture. He is too big to fit into any such narrow mold. Pilate referred to Him as the King of the Jews, but Jesus' own favorite title was Son of man. It is a title borrowed from the Book of Daniel and is used time and time again in the Gospels. It is intended to portray Jesus as the universal man with a universal appeal, the head of an entirely new humanity. This became abundantly clear when, following the Resurrection, Jesus said, "All power in heaven and in earth is given unto me" (Mt 28:18).

The earliest and simplest creed of the church was summed up in four words, "Jesus Christ is Lord" (Ph 2:11). The early church understood the phrase in its widest connotation. Jesus Christ is not only the Head of the church; He is also the Lord of history and the King of nations. He is the one and only Lord. He stands in a class by Himself. He occupies a solitary throne. Sooner or later all men must come to terms with Him (Jn 5:28–29) and all nations, large and small, must own His sway (Rev 11:15). He is the Son of God who, in the Incarnation, became the Son of man, that through His death, resurrection, and ascension, He might become the only Savior and Sovereign of the world (1 Tim 6:15). And the day is coming when every knee will bow and every tongue will confess that Jesus Christ is Lord to the glory of God the Father (Ph 2:10–11).

For the World Christian the lordship of Christ is not simply a beautiful prospect that will be realized in all its fullness only at the Second Coming. Rather, it is something to be experienced here and now in our daily occupation. Everything the Christian has belongs to Christ and is, therefore, at his disposal—his person, his possessions, his talents, even his vocation. Whether he becomes a missionary or a merchant, a preacher or a plumber, an engineer or an entrepreneur, will be determined by Christ, not by himself.

Raymond Lull, the first and greatest missionary to the Muslims, after selling all his property and possessions, dedicated himself to the service of Christ with these words: "To Thee, O Lord God, I offer myself, my children, and all that I possess. May it please Thee to accept all that I give to Thee, that I, and my wife and children, may be Thy lowly servants."

In a similar vein, David Livingstone, on his fifty-ninth birthday, after a lifetime of incredible hardship and privation in Central Africa, wrote in his diary, "My Jesus, my King, my life, my all; I again dedicate my whole self to Thee. Accept me and grant that ere this year is gone I may finish my task." The World Christian will not find it difficult to identify with Lull or Livingstone. These will be his sentiments too.

The Cosmopolitan Composition of the Church

A World Christian is one who recognizes the cosmopolitan composition of the church. The world into which Jesus came was a divided one. The Greeks, on the basis of culture, divided the world into two groups— Greeks and barbarians. The Romans, on the basis of politics, divided the world into two groups—citizens and slaves. The Jews, on the basis of religion, divided the world into two groups—Jews and Gentiles. If a person had the misfortune to be a barbarian, or a slave, or a Gentile, he was beyond the pale and doomed to be a second-class person as long as he lived.

Jesus adamantly refused to endorse such arbitrary, manmade distinctions. At best, they were discriminatory; at worst, they were downright destructive. Jesus came to seek and to save the lost, and they were to be found in all races and cultures. For obvious reasons His first offer of the kingdom was made to the Jews, but He never intended that the kingdom should be restricted to that people. He scandalized the self-righteous Pharisees by fraternizing with publicans and sinners. He incurred the wrath of the hierarchy by exposing their hypocrisy. He raised the ire of His fellow townsmen by making honorable mention of two Gentiles in Old Testament history. And when He died, He was fittingly placed between two malefactors, one of whom He saved—His last majestic act before He expired.

The apostles took their cue from Him. They preached a new gospel based on two fundamental facts: God loved the world and Christ died for all. And they practiced what they preached. If God loved the Greco-Roman world with all its sin, debauchery, and licentiousness, they would do the same. If Christ died for all, they would gladly open their doors to Jews and Gentiles, scribes and Pharisees, priests and Levites, rabbis and zealots—any and all who would embrace the faith.

It is true that they took some time to come to this conclusion, but Peter led the way after his vision of the sheet let down from heaven (Acts 10). To Cornelius he said, "I most certainly understand now that God is not one to show partiality, but in every nation the man who fears Him and does what is right, is welcome to Him" (Acts 10:34–35).

From then on the early church flung its doors open to all kinds and conditions of people.

It is noteworthy thatthe disciples were first called Christians in Antioch, the most cosmopolitan city in the Roman Empire, and the church was as cosmopolitan as the city. In similar manner, the little mission church in Philippi was a microcosm of the church universal. Among its charter members were three persons with little or nothing in common—the jailor, Lydia, and the slave girl. The jailor, doubtless, was a callous, uncouth Roman without faith or feeling until the gospel reached him. Lydia was an aristocratic, prosperous businesswoman, equally at home in commerce or culture. The slave girl was a poor, demented youngster who belonged body and soul to her unscrupulous masters, whose sole purpose in life was to make money. All three of them found the other two when they found Christ; together they formed the nucleus of Paul's favorite church, the church that brought him the most joy and gave him the greatest support. When writing to the Christians in Philippi he thanked God for their fellowship in the gospel from the very first day (Ph 1:3–5).

Michael Green, in *Let the Earth Hear His Voice,* has this to say about the cosmopolitan character of the early church:

> Master and slave ate together. Jew and Gentile ate together; unparalleled in the ancient world. Their fellowship was so vital that their leaders could be drawn from different races and cultures and colors and classes. Here was a fellowship in Christ which transcended all natural barriers. There was nothing like it anywhere—and there isn't still.[1]

Alas, we must confess that the church in the United States has not lived up to these high standards. It is still the most segregated institution in the country. Indeed, there are

---

1. J. D. Douglas, ed., *Let the Earth Hear His Voice* (Minneapolis: World Wide Publications, 1975), p. 175.

Christians who believe that segregation is ordained by God and any attempt to mix the races is frowned upon. The World Christian is not among that number. He sincerely believes that the church is by definition a cosmopolitan institution, and that its membership should be open to all and sundry regardless of their racial origin.

The Priority of World Missions

A World Christian is one who recognizes the absolute priority of world missions. The average evangelical church is a busy place, with many activities going on at the same time. Children, teen-agers, young people, college students, singles, married couples, and senior citizens all clamor for attention. Each group jealously guards its place in the program and its share of the budget.

The World Christian will recognize the legitimacy of these activities. They are a proper part of any active church's program. However, they are not an end in themselves, but a means to an end. The chief task of the church is not to keep its members happy, but to make them holy; to bring them to that degree of spiritual maturity that will permit them to function effectively as witnesses to the truth and power of the gospel (Eph 4:16). Only then can they become vessels meet for the Master's use and prepared unto every good work (2 Tim 2:21).

The World Christian then will make no apology for insisting on the priority of world missions. He will heartily agree with John E. Skoglund when he states, "Church and mission are one, and cannot in any way be broken apart. To break them apart is to make both cripples. . . . It [mission] is *the* mark of the church. And all other marks, if legitimate, are but explication of mission."[2]

Accordingly, mission is not something extraneous to the church. It is part of her nature, and when she has been true

2. John E. Skoglund, *To the Whole Creation: The Church Is Mission* (Valley Forge, Penn.: Judson, 1962), p. 94.

to her own genius she has always been a witnessing community. On the contrary, when she has lost her missionary vision she has turned inward and gone into decline. But whenever she has experienced revival she has always resumed her essential task—world missions.

The rationale for world missions is not found in two or three isolated texts of the Bible. It runs like a golden thread throughout Scripture, from Genesis to Revelation. James S. Stewart summed it up as well as anybody. He said, "There is no argument for mission. The entire action of God in history, the whole revelation of God in Christ— that is the argument."[3]

The Universal Scope of Christian Mission

A World Christian is one who recognizes the universal scope of the Christian mission. The American viewpoint *vis-à-vis* world affairs tends to be myopic. This comes out most clearly in our newspapers. The *Chicago Tribune* considers itself to be the "world's greatest newspaper," but its treatment of world events is extremely selective. It is much more interested in murders and muggings in Chicago than in what happens in Paris or Peking or even the United Nations. When Iran holds 52 Americans hostage for 444 days, or when the Soviet Union shoots down an unarmed civilian plane with 269 passengers (many of them Americans) on board, then our newspapers give us a daily, blow-by-blow account of what is happening. But once the crisis is resolved, the newspapers go back to business as usual with very little international news.

Europeans and Canadians coming to this country complain that they read almost nothing of their countries in our newspapers. Luigi Barzini, veteran journalist and former member of the Italian Parliament, was asked about Americans' understanding of foreign affairs. He replied:

---

3. James S. Stewart, *Thine Is the Kingdom* (New York: Scribner, 1957), p. 11.

The trouble is that foreign affairs in the United States is a matter for specialists. If you go to the provinces, people are not interested. I was in Cleveland, Ohio, not long ago. I opened the paper in the morning, and there was almost nothing in it about the world, about Europe, even about U.S. foreign policy. The result is that the country as a whole lives its own life with little awareness of the consequences some of its decisions may have on others.[4]

Unfortunately the same attitude prevails in many segments of the American church. When it comes to Christian activity there are four concentric circles of interest. The inner circle represents the local church; the second, the denomination; the third, the denomination's work overseas; and the fourth, the wider interests of the kingdom in all parts of the world.

The interest of many church members is pretty well confined to the activities of the local church, and they think they are doing well if they assume some responsibility in that restricted area. A few go farther and embrace in their thoughts the outreach of the denomination in the United States. A still smaller number, usually the members of the missionary committee, know anything about overseas missions. As for the fourth circle, it is either unknown or ignored, except at ecumenical gatherings; and there it is more often equated with church union rather than world mission.

The World Christian will not be content with this sad state of affairs. He is painfully aware of the melancholy fact that after two thousand years of church history, two-thirds of the world is still without a knowledge of Jesus Christ. He knows, of course, that the Christian mission rightly begins in Jerusalem; but he also knows that for too long a time we have been content to minister primarily to our Jerusalem. He deplores the fact that a large majority of full-time Christian workers are located in North America, where churches abound and where the Bible is the

4. *U.S. News and World Report*, June 7, 1982, p. 28.

best seller year after year. He knows and deplores the fact that as far as world evangelization is concerned, we are not even keeping up with the increase in population.

It is for these reasons that he believes in, and is totally committed to, the evangelization of the world. He will not, he cannot, rest until every member of the human race has had a clear presentation of the gospel. To this end he is prepared to devote all his powers of body, mind, and heart.

Personal Responsibility for World Missions

A World Christian is one who recognizes his own personal responsibility for world missions. By his attitude, understanding, and commitment he will be personally and vitally involved in home and foreign mission work. This does not mean that he will necessarily become a full-time, professional missionary. He may never go overseas. That is beside the point.

Being a World Christian is not a part-time profession, or a token gesture, or a passing hobby. Nor is it solely a matter of a faith promise at the annual missionary conference, or signing a check once a month, or writing the occasional letter to a missionary in Africa, though certainly a World Christian will do these things. It is a total commitment to all aspects of the Great Commission as outlined by Christ. It is total identification with God in the outworking of his redemptive purpose for the world for which Christ died.

There are a hundred-and-one ways in which a World Christian can get involved in world missions without even leaving his homeland.

I have a friend, now retired, who graduated from Ontario Bible College a long time ago. She applied to the China Inland Mission but was turned down for health reasons. Was that the end of her involvement in missions? Hardly. For the past 50 years she has devoted most of her time and effort, and not a little of her income, to world missions. She organized, and for 40 years led, several missionary prayer meetings each month in her neighborhood. She carried on a steady correspondence with hundreds of missionaries all over the world. She received their prayer letters, duplicated them, and sent them all over the country. In her modest little home she had a "prophet's chamber" where she entertained scores of missionaries every year. The walls of her living room, hall, and bedrooms were covered with pictures and paintings from the mission field. Bureaus, bookcases, and tables were decorated with mementos left by grateful missionaries.

Now in her seventies, she can no longer engage in these activities, but her heart still beats for missions. She never got to the mission field, even for a visit, but she probably accomplished more for the cause of Christ than many who did. When the awards are handed out for missionary service, I feel sure that my friend will be at the head of the receiving line. She is a classic example of a World Christian at work.

As I minister in churches all over the country I come across hundreds of lay people, women as well as men, who are personally involved in some aspect of world missions. They have never had any theological training, nor have they ever lived abroad; but they have a heart for world missions. It is the thing in which they are most interested. It is the cause to which they devote much of their time, thought, energy, and money.

8

Growing as a World Christian

Two of the distinguishing marks of life are growth and reproduction. This is true of all forms of life—vegetable, animal, and human. The human organism is born, matures, reproduces, and then dies. If at any point along the way the process of maturation is interrupted, the health of the organism deteriorates, sometimes even to the point of death. This is true in the spiritual as well as the physical realm. It is for this reason that the apostle Peter admonished the believers of his day to "grow in the grace and knowledge of our Lord and Savior Jesus Christ" (2 Pet 3:18). The believer seldom stands still in his spiritual life. Either he goes forward or he falls back.

The same is true of the World Christian. He does not became a World Christian overnight. There are certain things he will want to do to become a World Christian in the true sense of the term. Three of them are important.

Increase His Knowledge of World Affairs

One would imagine that since the world has become a global village, and almost every home has a television set and therefore has daily access to world news, that Americans would be among the best-informed people in the world.

149

Such is not the case. In fact, the opposite is true. In spite of the many advantages that we have, we are among the most poorly informed people in the world. The average American, including college graduates, knows very little about the world beyond our shores. Our knowledge of world affairs is embarrassingly meager. Others know much more about us than we know about them.

Our size is partially responsible for this melancholy state of affairs. We are the most powerful country in the United Nations, and assume that because we are large and strong that others will know about us. We feel no obligation to learn about them.

Take geography, for instance. Our ignorance of this field is abysmal. On one occasion, I asked 54 students in one of my seminary classes how many provinces there are in Canada. Only 4 knew the right answer—ten! On another occasion I went to the post office to mail a copy of a book to a friend in Singapore. The clerk behind the counter did not know the cost of the postage, so she consulted one of the large directories. She turned the pages one way, then turned them the other. She did everything but turn the directory upside down! I asked her what the problem was.

She replied, "I can't find 'Singapore.'"

"Where are you looking?" I inquired.

"I'm looking under 'Africa,'" she replied!

There are three good reasons the World Christian will want to increase his knowledge of world affairs.

In the first place, this world is God's world. He made it in the beginning, and lo these millions—or is it billions?—of years He has sustained it. It is to this planet that He sent His Son. It was on this planet that Jesus lived, died, and rose again. It was from this planet that He ascended into heaven, and it is to this planet that He will return to set up His kingdom. This world is the object of God's love, the recipient of His grace. It is His intention to save the world, not destroy it. The World Christian cannot afford to be ignorant of a world in which God has such an enormous investment.

A second reason the World Christian will want to increase his knowlege of world affairs is hinted at by Carlos Romulo, one-time Philippine ambassador to the United States, in a speech to the National Press Club in Washington. Said he:

It makes little difference whether the penguins of Antarctica know anything about the squirrels of Rock Creek Park. But it makes all the difference in the world whether the American people understand the crowded millions who inhabit Asia. Your destiny, Asia's destiny, the world's very survival, may depend on such an understanding on your part.[1]

The World Christian will want to gather every scrap of information he can about the human situation in all parts of the world. He is concerned when he reads about a famine in India, an earthquake in Guatemala, a tidal wave in Bangladesh, refugees in Pakistan, civil war in Nigeria, wars of liberation in Central America, martial law in Poland, mass executions in Iran, to say nothing of unrelieved poverty, hunger, and disease in all parts of the world.

The World Christian cannot go blithely on his way unconcerned for the well-being of his fellow men in other parts of the world. He knows that the human family is one and what happens in one part of the world is likely to affect the destiny of millions of persons in other parts of the world. No man lives to himself. No nation lives to itself. If the human race is to survive, we must recognize the interdependence of peoples and nations throughout the world. War in one part of the world can spread to other parts. When the economy of the United States goes into decline the economies of Europe follow in quick order. If oil from the Middle East were to be cut off, much of the industry in Europe and Japan would grind to a halt, and even in the United States the situation would become precarious.

---

1. *Asian Student,* January 27, 1957.

No nation, not even our own, is strong enough to survive on its own. For better or worse, our fate is bound up with the fate of the world. Our responsibility is particularly great since the United States has the ability to destroy civilization in a holocaust, the results of which stagger the imagination.

Whether or not he agrees with our government's foreign policy, military strategy, or economic system, the World Christian will want to invoke God's grace and guidance on our leaders in Washington and our ambassadors overseas. As a responsible citizen of the most powerful country in the world, he will want to think, act, plan, and pray intelligently, and in his own modest way make his contribution, however small, to peace, justice, and stability throughout the world.

Thirdly, the World Christian should increase his knowledge of world affairs because the Christian church, of which he is a member, is a worldwide institution, and some of his brothers and sisters in other parts of the world are living under conditions he would find intolerable. They need his prayers—and need them desperately. But he cannot pray intelligently unless he knows something about the social, economic, and political conditions under which they live. For example, what is the prime concern of the Christians in Hong Kong? Surely it is the prospect that the People's Republic of China will annex Hong Kong when Great Britain's lease expires in 1997. What is the prime concern of the Christians in Ethiopia? Surely it is the famine in the northern part of the country that has brought the people to the brink of starvation. What is the prime concern of the Christians in the Soviet Union? Surely it is the problem of how to give religious instruction to their own children in the home without having the children taken away and placed in an institution, or of having the father sent to Siberia.

There is no way that the World Christian can pray intelligently for these and other Christians without knowing something of the situation in which they find themselves.

In a word, one cannot be a World Christian without a working knowledge of the world, its geography, history, politics, religions, and economics.

In becoming properly informed, the World Christian will have to depend on his own interest and initiative. As we have already noted, the educational system will not do much for him. Nor will the average urban newspaper. Until very recently the quality of education in this country has been deteriorating year after year. Fewer and fewer schools, including colleges, are requiring foreign languages either for matriculation or graduation. Some 23 percent of our high-school graduates are said to be functional illiterates.

The World Christian deplores this dismal state of affairs, and is prepared, at least in his own case, to do what he can to remedy the situation. He will see to it that he has access to one of the better daily newspapers, such as the *New York Times,* the *Washington Post,* or the *Christian Science Monitor,* and he will be sure to read those sections designed to enlarge his knowledge of world affairs. In addition, he will want to read at least one weekly news magazine: *Time, Newsweek,* or the *U.S. News and World Report.*

Broaden His View of the Christian Church

The average church member has a woefully inadequate view of the Christian church. He tends to equate the kingdom of God with his church or denomination; with the result that he is a Presbyterian first and a Christian second, or a Methodist first and a Christian second, or a Baptist first and a Christian second.

I remember quite vividly an experience I had some years ago when I lived in Rhode Island. My wife and I were engaged one Sunday afternoon in a religious canvass of the community, inviting nonchurch folks to visit our church. At one house I introduced myself, as usual, as a member of the Barrington Baptist Church and explained that we were trying to contact any nonchurch folks who might be in the community. I was startled by the response. The woman, obviously a person of culture, stood erect, threw back her head, and said, rather emphatically, "I am an Episcopalian—and I hate the Baptists!" Then she went on to enlarge on the glories of the Episcopal Church.

I don't think there was any malice in her statement. She didn't really *hate* the Baptists. Her statement was just a dramatic way of underscoring her strong allegiance to her own denomination. However, I did get the impression that she was of the opinion that to be a Christian is indeed to be an Episcopalian, and that all other Christians are second-class citizens.

I trust that the reader will not misunderstand me at this point. I am not against denominations. I belong to one, and I support it faithfully with my gifts and prayers. However, there is something bigger, finer, and better than my denomination—the kingdom of God, of which even the largest denomination is but a small part. In the divided state of Christendom denominations serve a useful purpose. In spite of our best efforts at church union, they will probably be with us to the end. I don't think, however, that they will survive the Rapture. When we get to heaven denominational labels will fall away and we will all be brethren—spelled with a small *b*.

I had the privilege of serving in China for fifteen years, from 1935 to 1950, with the China Inland Mission, now the Overseas Missionary Fellowship. The CIM was an international, interdenominational mission of more than 1,300 workers from all the major denominations, from the Plymouth Brethren to the Episcopalians. For years these workers labored side by side, sometimes without ever knowing the denominational affiliation of their closest colleagues. The task of evangelizing one-quarter of the human race was so massive that somehow denominational loyalties did not loom very large. And the churches we brought into existence were free to determine their own church polity. It worked beautifully. We understood what the psalmist meant when he said, "Behold, how good and how pleasant it is for brothers to dwell together in unity" (Ps 133:1). It is instructive to note that the churches in China, now free of missionary control, have done away with denominational labels. The churches are simply known as Christian churches; for the very first time Christianity is no longer regarded as a "foreign religion."

I shall always be grateful to God that He allowed me to live and move in interdenominational circles most of my life. I should hate to be placed in a denominational straitjacket. I have always felt free to go wherever I was invited. There were some churches, of course, where I was not welcome. For some, I was too conservative. For others, I was too liberal. For still others, I did not have the "proper" credentials. But wherever I have gone my soul has been refreshed, my fellowship has been enriched, and my sympathies have been enlarged by a wider fellowship. Paul could say, "All things belong to you, whether Paul or Apollos or Cephas or the world or life or death or things present or things to come; all things belong to you, and you belong to Christ; and Christ belongs to God" (1 Cor 3:21–23).

Naturally, John Wesley sustains a unique relationship to Methodists, but certainly he does not "belong" to them. They have no monopoly on him. He is just too big for that. The same is true for John Calvin, John Darby, John Knox, or Martin Luther. I like to think that they all belong to me! I read their works, I rejoice in their deeds, and I fellowship with their followers; and I am greatly enriched thereby.

For 13 years it was my joy to teach at Trinity Evangelical Divinity School in Deerfield, Illinois. Trinity is a denominational school, established and maintained by the Evangelical Free Church of America; but one can be on the campus for three months and never hear, in chapel or classroom, any mention of the Evangelical Free Church! Only 30 percent of the freshmen are Evangelical Free. The same is true of about 50 percent of the faculty. On the other hand, there are other seminaries in the country where

156 The Response: The World Christians We Must Be

every student and every faculty member is required to be a
member of the supporting denomination. In such an environment it would be difficult for the student to develop
an adequate appreciation or understanding of the church
universal.

The World Christian, therefore, deplores the policy
which says, "Methodist money for Methodist missions," or
"Presbyterian preachers for Presbyterian pulpits," or
"Lutheran students for Lutheran seminaries." That's just
too narrow for him. He wants to be free to fellowship with
all these groups, to minister to them and have them minister to him.

Who ever thinks of E. Stanley Jones as a Methodist, or
D. L. Moody as a Congregationalist, or Billy Graham as a
Southern Baptist? These men are just too big to have a
denominational label hung around their necks. They belong to their own denominations all right; but in a truer
sense they belong to the church at large, and are claimed
by all who have an interest in the proclamation of the
gospel and the extension of the kingdom around the world.

If Wesley were here today it is doubtful that he would
confine his ministry to Methodist churches. He boasted
that the world was his parish, and indeed it was. He said on
one occasion: "If your heart beats with my heart in love
and loyalty to Jesus Christ, give me your hand." I like that.
That is the true basis of ecumenicity. What we have in
common in Christ is greater than the many lesser things
that divide us. The litmus test of Christian fellowship is
not what you think of Billy Graham, or Oral Roberts, or
Robert Schuller, or the Revised Standard Version, or the
charismatic movement. These are the petty things that
are dividing the children of God in our day. The real test is
the same as it has always been: "What do you think of
Christ? Whose Son is He?" That is still the question to be
asked and answered. In the first century the earliest
Christian creed comprised four words: Jesus Christ is
Lord. Jesus was His name as the Son of man. Christ was
His title as the Son of God. The first speaks of His true

humanity, the second of His true deity. We confess Him as our one and only Lord. He is the Head of the church and we are all members of His body..

The World Christian may never have the privilege of being a member of an ecumenical organization, but he will always embrace in his plans and prayers the whole household of God, knowing that every denomination includes brothers and sisters who know and love the same Lord he does.

Deepen His Understanding of the Christian Mission

In seeking to understand the mission of the church, it is a good idea to begin with Jesus' last words. In the Great Commission He commanded His followers to go into all the world, preach the gospel to every creature, and make disciples of all nations. It is fair to ask: How are we doing? Are we winning or losing the battle? Are we gaining ground or losing ground? Is the number of Christians in the world increasing or decreasing?

If we go back to the time of William Carey (the 1790s), regarded by many as the father of modern missions, we discover that the Christian church was pretty much confined to the North Atlantic community. Apart from Egypt, Ethiopia, and South Africa, there were no churches in the great continent of Africa. In Asia, there were no churches except a few Orthodox churches in the Levant and South India and several small Protestant churches in the Netherlands East Indies (now Indonesia). The rest of Asia and Africa was without a Christian church.

How different is the situation today. Apart from a few Muslim countries, such as Mauritania and Somalia, there are growing, thriving churches in nearly 50 countries of Black Africa; new converts are embracing Christianity at the rate of 20,000 per day. In Asia there are large and thriving churches in India, Burma, Indonesia, the Philippines, and Korea, and smaller but growing churches in most of the other countries.

Indeed, most of the church growth that is taking place today is occurring in the Third World. And if the present pattern of growth continues for another two decades, by the end of the century the Christian church will be a predominantly colored church. On the other hand, before we give way to self-congratulation, we should realistically face up to the fact that in spite of our gargantuan efforts we are not keeping up with the population growth. Obviously we are not winning the world.

The World Christian will want to know the facts—good and bad—and then plan, work, and pray accordingly. He will want to know which countries are open and which are closed to Christian missionaries. He will want to know how the church is faring in such Communist countries as the Soviet Union, Cuba, Ethiopia, Vietnam, North Korea, Angola, and Mozambique. He will be equally concerned for the struggling churches in such Muslim countries as Bangladesh, Pakistan, Malaysia, Egypt, Iran, Jordan, and Syria. He will certainly want to get the encouraging facts concerning the growth of the church in the People's Republic of China since the Great Proletarian Cultural Revolution (1966–69).

He will want to know why it has been so difficult to win converts in Asia and so easy to do the same in Africa. He will want to understand the role of medicine and education in the overall missionary enterprise. He will want to be acquainted with some of the new and exciting developments during this postwar period—the Pentecostal movement in Latin America, Theological Education by Extension in Africa and Latin America, and the Church Growth Movement in all parts of the world. And last but not least, he will want to learn about the most exciting phenomenon of all—the rapid increase in the number of Third World missionaries.

And how is he to acquire all this knowledge? It will not be enough to attend and support the annual missionary conference in his church. He will have to do some good, hard study on his own; but the rewards will be commensurate with the effort. In a word, he will become a *student of missions*, in which capacity he will want to read as many books and periodicals as he can. Once he gets into this field of study, he will discover no lack of reliable, up-to-date material. Fifty years ago a book on missions was an event. Today such books are tumbling off the presses in such numbers that one has neither the money to buy them nor the time to read them all!

I would suggest that he begin by making a study of the worldwide outreach of his own denomination. The United Presbyterians and the United Church of Christ both publish an annual *Prayer Calendar* or *Prayer Directory* which lists the name and address of every missionary. The Southern Baptists have their missionary monthly, *The Commission*, without doubt the finest of its kind in North America, if not the world. Other denominations, large and small, have their house organs which usually devote some space to world missions.

If he wants to go beyond his own denomination—and he surely will—then he should subscribe to such non-denominational magazines as *World Vision, World Christian, Missionary News Service, Pulse,* and other fine periodicals. If he really wants to get his teeth into missiological studies, he will find the *International Review of Mission, Evangelical Missions Quarterly, Missiology,* and the *International Bulletin of Missionary Research* extremely helpful. For students, there is nothing better than *World Christian* and the new *International Journal of Frontier Missions.*

The list of good books is almost endless. Some of the more prominent books will be found in the bibliography of this book. A few are so relevant for the World Christian that I also list them here: *In the Gap* by David Bryant, *On the Crest of the Wave* by C. Peter Wagner, and *Today's Tentmakers* by J. Christy Wilson, Jr. From time to time the secular news magazines carry articles on the Christian church and religion. *Time,* in its December 27, 1982, issue had a missionary, Leon Dillinger, on the front cover! And the lead article was entitled "The New Missionary." For a secular magazine it was an exceptionally fine and fair article. Many of the well-known evangelical periodicals, such as *Eternity* and *Christianity Today,* frequently carry articles relating to church and mission around the world. Others, such as *Moody Monthly,* have a whole department devoted to missions.

If the World Christian lives up to his name, he will believe that the prime responsibility of the church is the evangelization of the world. He will also believe that this responsibility devolves not just on the pastors, missionaries, and other full-time workers, but on every member of the Christian community. To this end, he will devote a goodly share of his time and energy. With the passing of time he will enlarge his knowledge of missions at home and overseas until he can teach a Sunday-school class with at least as much expertise as that of a missionary on furlough. He will also be a welcome resource person on the missionary committee of his local church. And certainly he will be a joy to the heart of his pastor.

A person is not likely to develop into a World Christian overnight. It will take time and effort. Perhaps a good way to begin would be to select eight or ten passages of Scripture that deal with God's sovereign plan of salvation, and meditate on them until they become part and parcel of one's thinking. The following passages will prove helpful as a beginning.

> O Lord, our Lord,
> How majestic is Thy name in all the earth. [Ps 8:1]

> The earth is the Lord's, and all it contains,
> The world, and those who dwell in it. [Ps 24:1]

> "For God so loved the world, that He gave His only begotten Son, that whoever believes in Him should not perish, but have eternal life." [Jn 3:16]

The Father has sent the Son to be the Savior of the world. [1 Jn 4:14]

God was in Christ reconciling the world to Himself. [2 Cor 5:19]

"This gospel of the kingdom shall be preached in the whole world for a witness to all the nations." [Mt 24:14]

"Go into all the world and preach the gospel to all creation" [Mk 16:15] . . . "and make disciples of all the nations." [Mt 28:19]

> "Our Father who art in heaven,
> Hallowed be Thy name.
> Thy kingdom come.
> Thy will be done,
> On earth as it is in heaven." [Mt 6:9–10]

And the seventh angel sounded; and there arose loud voices in heaven, saying,
"The kingdom of the world has become the kingdom of our Lord, and of His Christ; and He will reign forever and ever." [Rev 11:15]

Memorize these passages and repeat them to yourself at least once a day—slowly, deliberately, thoughtfully, and prayerfully for a month; and you will begin to think as a World Christian, to plan and pray as a World Christian, to work and witness as a World Christian. And you will be well on your way to becoming a World Christian.

9

Sharing as a World Christian

The world says, "What I have, I hold." The Christian says, "What I have, I share." The two philosophies may be summed up in two words: get and give.

The world proceeds on the assumption that you go round only once, so go with gusto and grab all that you can. And don't be too scrupulous in the way you get it. In business, politics, and sports, competition is the order of the day. In sports, winning is everything. In business, the free-enterprise system often ends up in a dog-eat-dog situation. The big conglomerates get bigger and bigger and in the process push the little guy to the wall. In politics, it is even worse. There the winner takes all. If, along the way, the competition is eliminated, so what? That's the name of the game.

That may be the way of the world. It is not the Christian way. Jesus said, "It is more blessed to give than to receive" (Acts 20:35). He said, "Do good, and lend, expecting nothing in return" (Lk 6:35). He also warned that a man's life does not consist in the abundance of his possessions (Lk 12:15). E. Stanley Jones used to say, "If I have something that my brother needs more than I do, I'm duty bound as a Christian to let him have it." That's the Christian way.

The two best-known parables of Jesus are those about the prodigal son and the good Samaritan. Our liberal friends have taken the second very seriously and have tended to gloss over the first. We evangelicals have made much of the first and have neglected the second. Both are right in what they emphasize and both are wrong in what they overlook. Both parables were spoken by Jesus and form part of His essential teaching. We are not at liberty to choose one and forget the other. The gospel message of repentance and forgiveness in the parable of the Prodigal Son should never be neglected. The same is true of the humanitarian concern in the parable of the Good Samaritan. What God has put together, let no man, liberal or evangelical, put asunder.

According to Adolf Harnack the parable that most impressed the early Christians was the parable of the Sheep and the Goats in Matthew 25. He lists ten humanitarian services rendered by the church not only to its members but to outsiders as well: alms in general, support of teachers and officials, support of widows and orphans, support of the sick and infirm, the care of prisoners and convicts in the mines, the care of poor people needing burial, the care of slaves, providing disaster relief, furnishing employment, and finally, extending hospitality.[1]

Considering the paucity of their members and the meagerness of their resources, the early Christians did more for the amelioration of human suffering than did any succeeding generation of believers.

The World Christian will not want to be one step behind his first-century counterpart. Like his Master he will want to be a loving, caring, sharing person. There are several major things he will want to share.

Sharing His Faith

The World Christian believes that all men everywhere are lost and need to be saved. This goes for the "pagan" here at home just as much as it does for the "heathen"

---

1. Adolf Harnack, *The Mission and Expansion of Christianity in the First Three Centuries* (New York: Harper, 1962), p. 153.

overseas. He also believes that in order to be saved, one must hear and believe the gospel. And he believes that in the gospel of Christ, he possesses *the* truth concerning God, man, sin, and salvation.

This being so, the World Christian will want to begin by sharing his most precious possession—his faith. He will recognize that the greatest benefit he can confer on any member of the human race is to introduce that person to Jesus Christ. Far from regarding religion as a private matter, he will seek to share the greatest piece of news in today's news-weary world.

The World Christian will recognize that sharing the good news of the gospel is not solely the responsibility of a few full-time experts—pastors, missionaries, and others. It is the personal privilege and responsibility of every member of the church. He will call to mind that in the early church the work of evangelism was not confined to the apostles but was carried on by the rank and file of the church membership. Will Durant was right when he wrote, "Nearly every convert, with the ardor of a revolutionary, made himself an office of propaganda."[2]

Luke tells us in Acts 8 that when persecution scattered the early believers, they "went everywhere preaching the gospel." Indeed the church in Antioch, which ultimately supplanted Jerusalem as the "mother" church in the empire, was started by these "displaced persons" who "gossiped the gospel" wherever they went (Acts 11:19).

The World Christian, whether at home or abroad, on an errand of business or pleasure, will regard himself as an "office of propaganda" and take every opportunity to share his faith.

Sharing His Goods

Sharing as a World Christian involves much more than sharing one's faith, important as that is. There are other

2. Will Durant, *Caesar and Christ: A History of Roman Civilization and of Christianity from Their Beginnings to A.D. 325* (New York: Simon and Schuster, 1944), p. 602.

things to be shared. One of them is his possessions. Here again the World Christian will take his cue from the early Christians. Speaking of the first believers in Jerusalem Luke says, "All those who had believed were together, and had all things in common" (Acts 2:44). A second and fuller reference to this practice is made in Acts 4:32: "And the congregation of those who believed were of one heart and soul; and not one of them claimed that anything belonging to him was his own; but all things were common property to them."

They not only shared their savings; they shared their capital as well. "For there was not a needy person among them, for all who were owners of land or houses would sell them and bring the proceeds of the sales, and lay them at the apostles' feet; and they would be distributed to each, as any had need" (Acts 4:34–35).

That this practice was not confined to Jerusalem in the first years of the Christian era is seen in the apostle John's admonition at least a generation or two later. Said he, "Whoever has the world's goods, and beholds his brother in need and closes his heart against him, how does the love of God abide in him?" (1 Jn 3:17). Love to be pure must be practical. John goes on to say, "Little children, let us not love with word or with tongue, but in deed and truth" (1 Jn 3:18).

James, in his epistle, is even more emphatic. "What use is it, my brethren, if a man says he has faith, but he has no works? Can that faith save him? If a brother or sister is without clothing and in need of daily food, and one of you says to them, 'Go in peace, be warmed and be filled,' and yet you do not give them what is necessary for their body, what use is that? Even so faith, if it has no works, is dead" (Ja 2:14–17).

The World Christian, then, has a sound biblical basis for sharing his goods. He also has the example of the missionaries to spur him on. Most of them cheerfully give up many of the amenities of Western civilization to share the gospel with the peoples in the non-Christian part of the world.

This is particularly true of those who live and labor in the more primitive parts of the world such as the mountains of Irian Jaya or the jungles of the Amazon Basin. The missionaries of the nineteenth century often ended up by giving their lives as well as their goods. When the early pioneers went out they did not expect ever to return; and many of them didn't.

The World Christian will hold lightly to his possessions. He will readily acknowledge that he is a steward of the manifold grace of God; that everything he possesses has been given to him by God. And one day he will have to give an account of his stewardship. Nothing then will be too costly or too precious to share with friends, neighbors, or even strangers. His home, food, clothes, car, tools, books, household goods—everything will be at the disposal of those in need. He will hold back nothing.

Some Christians are reluctant to share their personal possessions because they are too expensive. The World Christian will not be swayed by such considerations. He will ask himself the question: Does a follower of Christ have the right to own something that is too valuable to share with others? He will conclude that if an article is too expensive to lend, it is too expensive to own.

Sharing His Time

Time is a very precious commodity. It is the stuff that life is made of. Waste your time and you waste your life.

Some people find it easier to share their goods than their time. They have plenty of the former, but have only a limited supply of the latter—168 hours a week to be exact. It is possible to "stretch" our dollars. There is no way we can "stretch" our time. This being so, it may be more difficult to share one's time than to share one's goods.

The average person devotes eight hours a day to work, and another eight hours to sleep. The remaining eight hours must be divided among travel, grooming, household chores, family responsibilities, and entertaining. This does not leave much time for recreation, hobbies, or friends, except on weekends. The average person does not have much leisure time.

The World Christian, however, will recognize that time is God's gift to him and should be used wisely. He will remember that in the Old Testament God required not only a tenth of the Israelite's wealth but also one-seventh of his time. It was called the Sabbath and on that day he was expected to refrain from all unnecessary labor and keep the day "holy unto the Lord."

It is true that we are no longer under law but under grace; but this does not mean that we are free to do exactly what we like with our time and money. God has a claim on both. If, under the law, the Israelite gave one-tenth of his income and one-seventh of his time, should not the Christian, under grace, do at least as much?

The World Christian will do his best to arrange his schedule in such a way that he will have some time each week to share with others. If he cannot "find" time, he will have to "make" time. He will begin by "making" time to be with his family on a regular basis. Christian service, like charity, begins at home. But he will not stop there. He will put forth a concentrated effort to respond to the needs of others beyond the family circle—friends, neighbors, business associates, church members, community people. To help any of them will always require time. There are all kinds of organizations to which he can devote his time— the church, the choir, the Sunday school, the youth group, the Awana Boys, the missionary committee, the Parent-Teachers Association, the Rotary Club, the United Fund, and a host of other service organizations found in any city of any size.

When he travels abroad—something many executives do these days—he will have an opportunity to see church and mission work firsthand. On the evenings and on weekends when he is free he will go out of his way to contact the missionaries and through them be introduced to church and mission work in various parts of the world. I knew of an employee of Baxter Travenol who found himself in Mexico City over a long weekend with nothing to do and nowhere to go. He had never been so bored in all his life. Next time he went to Mexico I gave him the name and address of a missionary in that city. He called the missionary on the phone and introduced himself. The missionary picked him up late Friday night, entertained him in his home, and spent the weekend introducing him to various missions and churches in the city. The man was so thrilled with what he saw that when he made his next trip to Europe he wanted the names and addresses of missionaries in the cities he planned to visit. Now wherever he goes he makes it a point to contact the missionaries and through them get a glimpse of the Lord's work.

Christian doctors and dentists in increasing numbers are giving time to active missionary work on a short-term basis. Some spend their annual vacation overseas in a mission hospital performing delicate operations that are beyond the competence of the local missionaries. I have friends who have spent several vacations in this way.

Sharing His Talents

Every Christian has *some* talents. There are two kinds of talent—the natural talents with which we are born and the spiritual gifts or talents given to the believer by the Holy Spirit. Both kinds of talent can be used in the service of Christ. In addition there are skills that can be acquired—accountancy, computer science, teaching, writing, music, carpentry, masonry, plumbing, bricklaying, and a host of other mental and manual skills. All such skills are in great demand on the mission field, either on a long-term or a short-term basis.

The May 1984 Wycliffe Associates *Newsletter* called for 141 volunteers for construction. Wanted were carpenters, plumbers, electricians, bricklayers, painters, and helpers of all kinds in nine locations: Dallas, Central America, Papua New Guinea, Quebec, Cameroon, Ivory Coast, Kenya, the Philippines, and South America. Some projects lasted for three months, others six. Roy and Ruby Grove of Hagerstown, Maryland, helped build apartments at Waxhaw, North Carolina. They wrote, "We spent our vacation there this year. Ruby worked in the kitchen while Roy worked as a carpenter's helper. We've been on two other WA jobs and are planning to be involved in upcoming projects. We encourage others to be involved too."

Today there are all kinds of voluntary services available to the World Christian at home and overseas. In 1983 volunteers donated 9,218 hours, valued at $57,053, in MAP International's Wheaton and South American offices. These volunteers assisted in handling correspondence and offered consultancy services in data processing and communications, among other things. These people are now part of the MAP Volunteer Network.

Other organizations have similar programs, among them the Mennonite Central Committee and Men for Missions of the OMS International. With international jet travel safe, swift, and comparatively cheap, it is relatively easy for World Christians to spend a month or a summer or even a year in missionary work overseas. They can even enter countries such as Nepal and Afghanistan that are closed to professional missionaries.

Sharing His Wealth

Billy Sunday used to say that the last part of a person to be converted is his pocketbook. One of the very best ways to gauge a Christian's dedication to the cause of Christ is to examine his checkbook. And the real test is not how much he has given away but how much he has left at the end of the month.

The Christian people of America owe an enormous debt to the other peoples of the world, and that for two good reasons. The average American family lives much better than its counterparts in other countries of the world. Second, many families in the Third World are unbelievably poor and there is little hope of their ever being able to better themselves, unless we in the more affluent part of the world are willing to share our wealth.

The poverty of many Third World countries beggars description. Not even television can adequately depict the deprivation of the rural peoples in India, Bangladesh, Haiti, and other countries. The average income per family of four in the United States is almost $20,000 a year. In scores of other countries it is about $1,000. Of course, $1,000 will go much farther in India than it will here. Even so the gap between the two standards of living is unacceptably large.

We usually divide the world into two camps—East and West. That division is based on politics. There is, however, another division—North and South—and that is based on economics. Americans are much more concerned with the division between East and West. The peoples in the Third World are much more conscious of the division between North and South. And in the long run, the second may turn out to be more dangerous than the first. It is difficult to imagine what it will be like if, following civil war throughout Central America, millions of impoverished refugees pour over the Rio Grande into Texas and New Mexico. It will make the invasion in 1984 of 125,000 "boat people" from Cuba look like a small weekend excursion.

Americans have a reputation for being generous, and most Americans enjoy the reputation. As a matter of fact, we are not as generous as we think we are—if our foreign-aid figures are any criterion. The Marshall Plan in the late 1940s was eminently successful. With $12 billion we pulled Western Europe out of the economic morass that followed World War II and helped to prepare the way for the amazing postwar boom that Germany and other countries have experienced.

Today, however, we are not nearly so generous with our foreign aid. The total cost of the Marshall Plan represented 2.79 percent of our Gross National Product at that time. Today our total foreign-aid program represents only .24 percent of GNP. On that basis 11 other countries are giving more than we are.

The poverty of the Third World is so horrendous that only a massive infusion of outside capital will solve the problems. In 1974 the developing countries in the United Nations proposed a "new international economic order." The affluent countries of the West were asked to devote 2 percent of their GNP to the economic development of the other countries. The proposal was rejected. And the problems remain.

The World Christian, by himself, will not be able to solve the economic problems of the world; but that is no excuse for inaction. There are some things he can do, and these he will want to do.

By regular, systematic giving he can make a difference. Usually a dollar invested overseas will go much farther than one invested here at home. It is possible to support an orphan with World Vision for $18 a month; that will provide food, clothing, and education. Such opportunities abound on the mission field. Every week I receive 10 to 20 letters appealing for money. In fact, occasionally they come so fast, I no sooner have my check in the mail than another request comes—from the same mission! Some people take offense at this and wish the missions would be less importunate in their appeals. Not the World Christian. He will not object to the many appeals that come his way. He may not be able to respond to all of them, but he will respond to as many as he can. And those to which he cannot respond will certainly have a place in his thoughts and prayers.

When it comes to giving, the World Christian will naturally give priority to his own denomination; but he will not stop there. He will want to support missionary work across the board and around the world. He will do his best to include various kinds of work in different regions of the world—Asia, Africa, Europe, Latin America, and the Middle East.

Someone might ask, "How can one person be expected to support missions on such a grand scale? After all, there are more than seven hundred sending and supporting agencies based in North America alone."

Much will depend on the person's income and interests. An individual with an income of $30,000 ought to be able to set aside $8,000 for the Lord. A family with an income of $50,000 ought to be able to live comfortably on $40,000 and give the remainder to Christian work. With that kind of money, the World Christian can afford to spread his giving around the world and still make a solid contribution to each mission.

And he should have no difficulty in locating missions to support. He will not have to go to them. They will come to him, and before long he will be inundated with appeals for help. At this point some people get angry; others are frustrated. Not the World Christian. He will appreciate the following statement that appeared on the cover of *Africa Now* some years ago: "If I get one more letter asking for money I will . . . [turn the page] . . . praise the Lord!"

To some extent he will be guided by his interests. Some donors prefer to concentrate on evangelism and church planting. They will want to support the Christian and Missionary Alliance, the Assemblies of God, the Evangelical Alliance Mission, the Overseas Missionary Fellowship, and others whose main work is in this area. Others are more interested in Bible translation and distribution. They will want to support the American Bible Society, Wycliffe Bible Translators, World Home Bible League, and the Pocket Testament League. Still others, with a deep concern for the physical and material needs of mankind, will want to give to MAP International and World Vision International. Still others may elect to support radio work and will direct their giving to Trans World Radio, World Radio Missionary Fellowship, and the Far

East Broadcasting Company. Others again may prefer to assist such technical agencies as Mission Aviation Fellowship or Gospel Recordings. Those interested in student work have several choices: Campus Crusade for Christ, Inter-Varsity Christian Fellowship, Navigators, and International Students, Inc.

Nor will the World Christian want to forget home missions, especially the educational institutions that are training missionary candidates—Bible colleges such as Moody, Columbia, Lancaster, Ontario, and Multnomah; and seminaries such as Trinity, Fuller, Dallas, Denver, Westminster, Gordon-Conwell, and others. Without their graduates, the supply of qualified missionary candidates would dry up in a few years.

Anyone wishing to get in touch with some of the many evangelical missons may write to the Interdenominational Foreign Mission Association, P. O. Box 395, Wheaton, Illinois 60187, the Evangelical Foreign Missions Association, 1430 K Street N. W., Washington, D.C. 20005, or the Fellowship of Missions, 4205 Chester Avenue, Cleveland, Ohio 44103. Together, these three associations account for more than 20,000 missionaries serving with 175 mission boards working in 130 countries of the world.

How is the World Christian to decide how to allocate his giving? I will tell you what I have found helpful.

At the beginning of the year I sit down and draw up a giving schedule. I estimate my annual income, decide what I can live on, and then set aside the remainder for the Lord's work. I take this last figure and divide it among some 20 or more home and foreign mission agencies. I decide how much I will give to each one and send it in on a quarterly basis. In this way, my giving for the entire year is planned ahead of time. When I get appeals from a mission on my list, I simply read the letter and pray about it, but do not give until that mission's turn comes round again in another month or two.

Of course, there are always one or two catastrophic needs that arise unexpectedly and for these I keep some funds in abeyance. Apart from cases of this sort, when the appeals arrive, I feel no great urge to give.

There are certain definite advantages to this plan:

1. It forces me to give serious thought to the way I spend the Lord's money.
2. It enables me to avoid compulsive giving.
3. I end up with a well-balanced support system, representing a cross section of evangelical missions at home and abroad.
4. I have the satisfaction of giving on a regular basis.
5. I avoid a guilt complex whenever I receive an appeal to which I make no response.
6. I can pray intelligently for at least 20 missionary agencies each week.

Churches as well as individuals can share their wealth. A good example is Eastminster Presbyterian Church in Wichita, Kansas, that launched a $525,000 building program shortly after a devastating earthquake demolished thousands of homes and buildings (many churches among them) in Guatemala. At a meeting of the board of elders a layman spoke up. "How can we set out to buy an ecclesiastical Cadillac when our brothers and sisters in Guatemala have just lost their little Volkswagen?" The elders agreed to modify their plans. They paid off the architect and settled for a modest $180,000 building. They then sent their pastor and two elders to Guatemala to ascertain how they could help the churches there to rebuild. The team reported back to the board of elders, whereupon the elders, with the enthusiastic support of the congregation, decided to borrow $120,000 from a local bank and to send the money to Guatemala to rebuild 26 churches and 28 pastors' houses.

Inspired by the example of Eastminster, another congregation modified its building plans and sent $60,000 to Guatemala. And churches in India, hearing about the project, raised $1,200 to help rebuild the churches in Guatemala.

Sharing His Home

It is said of the Englishman that his home is his castle. It is true of other people as well. Most Americans regard their home as private property to be used primarily if not exclusively for the benefit of the family members. Consequently hospitality is not nearly as common in the United States as it is in other parts of the world, such as the Far East and the Middle East, where hospitality is a way of life.

One problem is that our homes are smaller than they used to be when we were a predominantly agricultural nation. Farmers usually have large houses with plenty of room. Also, more than 50 percent of our women are now engaged in work outside the home, which means they have less time for entertaining. Moreover, recent expansion of the motel industry in all parts of the country tends to rob the home of its former importance as a place for entertaining Christian workers.

In contrast to our lack of hospitality, the New Testament portrays hospitality as a Christian virtue practiced widely in the early church. One qualification of elders was that they be "given to hospitality" (1 Tim. 3:2, KJV). The same expression is used in Romans 12:13 where Paul exhorts the believers in Rome to open their homes to fellow believers. Traveling evangelists and apostles frequently found a home away from home with Christian families. Displaced persons, fleeing from persecution, could expect to be received with kindness in the homes of their fellow Christians. In those days, hospitality was indeed a way of life.

Today's World Christian has a splendid opportunity to practice hospitality as a Christian virtue and thus extend the frontiers of the kingdom of God. There are in the United States today some 340,000 international students.

They come from every continent in the world. Many of them come from countries that are closed to Christian missionaries. Others come from countries where there is not a single organized indigenous church. Young people are the leaders of tomorrow, and when they return home, they will fill important positions in the political, professional, and business worlds. It is impossible to overestimate the strategic importance of such a large group of expatriates in our midst. Many of them become fast friends and when they return home they become ambassadors of goodwill. Alas, others return home to stir up anti-American sentiment. Much depends on how they are treated during their stay here. The coup that brought the Communists to power in Afghanistan in 1978 was planned by Afghan students at UCLA!

The vast majority of these international students experience culture shock as serious as anything encountered by missionaries going to Africa or Asia. They have to get used to our weather, our food, our manners, our morals, and a host of other things that we take for granted. They like our open society with all kinds of freedom, but they are shocked by some aspects of our culture—drugs, sex, violence, promiscuity, and pornography. Most of them are extremely lonesome, especially in the beginning. Even those who live on campus are lonely. Very few American students go out of their way to make the international students feel at home.

Nor have the Christian churches done much to meet the special needs of these strangers in our midst. Even the parachurch groups on campus seem to have largely bypassed these people. There are exceptions, of course. One church in Bellingham, Washington, has a full-time, fully-supported pastor who devotes all his time to the international students at the university in that city. International Students, Inc., a parachurch group on many campuses, is concerned exclusively with such students.

The World Christian will see in these friends an opportunity to influence the future course of Christian missions. There is no telling what these students might do for the cause of Christ when they return home, if only they come to know Him while they are here. Countries that are now closed to Western missionaries could conceivably open their doors if a Christian were to be appointed Minister of Immigration.

The foreign students in this country are interested in nearly everything we have to offer; they especially appreciate the privilege of visiting in our homes. After all, that is where they will see family life. Besides, they are accustomed to practicing hospitality back home and they miss it severely when they come here. To be invited to spend a weekend in one of our homes is something they will cherish. Even a Sunday dinner is a welcome diversion.

Probably the most difficult time for foreign students is vacation time. In some schools no provision is made for students who remain in the dormitories over the Christmas break. During those weeks students must fend for themselves, buying their own food and cooking their own meals—assuming they have access to cooking facilities. Quite often the dining room is closed. Sometimes even the dorms are closed. This works no great hardship on American students; but it is exceedingly difficult for foreign students, many of whom have nowhere to go unless a roommate invites them to spend Christmas with him at home.

Entertaining foreign students is not always easy. It takes time, patience, tact, understanding, and sensitivity if the student is to really feel at home and enjoy his stay. A Hindu should not be served beef and a Muslim should not be expected to eat pork. Both will be embarrassed if served alcoholic drinks.

International students are not the only ones who need a home away from home. Missionary kids, known as MKs, when they reach college age (sometimes high-school age) come to the United States for their education. Those who attend high school need a year-round home. Those in college usually live in the dorms, but they need hospitality over the Christmas holiday and during the summer vacation. Being separated from their children is the greatest sacrifice that missionaries have to make; and their concern for them is never greater than when they have to return to the field and leave their teen-age children at home. Providing a home for these young people is a much-needed ministry and one that is immensely appreciated by the parents—and the children. It is one more way for the World Christian to make a contribution to the cause of Christ around the world.

Missionaries on furlough form another group that needs hospitality. Locating suitable, affordable housing is one of the greatest problems facing missionaries on furlough. Houses are scarce, locations are often poor, and rents are high. Here is another opportunity for the World Christian to lend a helping hand. Not many families have the facilities to suddenly accommodate a family of four; but churches could do a better job than they have in the past. An increasing number of missionary-minded churches are investing in parsonages reserved for missionaries on furlough. The Southern Baptists are doing yeoman service in this respect. Some of the larger independent churches are also moving in this direction.

Dr. John Elsen and his wife, Virginia, are World Christians par excellence who have been practicing Christian hospitality for the last 35 years. Their story is told in the April 1982 issue of *Worldwide Challenge*, the house organ of Campus Crusade for Christ.

> Dr. John Elsen has been an ear, nose and throat specialist in Evanston, Ill., for 32 years. So why is he driving a 1972 Valiant with more than 100,000 miles on it? Why not a new Cadillac or a BMW? The Elsens' attitude toward their automobile reflects their life-style in general—one of giving for the cause of Christ.
>
> For almost 30 years the Elsens have opened their home to seemingly everybody. In recent months Dr. John and Aunt Ginny, as their many friends and guests call them, have

hosted students from local colleges, a missionary family from Zimbabwe, a family from Costa Rica, postdoctoral students from India, Spain, China and Egypt, and an elderly woman from church.

For 22 years the Elsens also owned a duplex near their house and rented it at cost to missionaries on furlough. In 1978 they gave it to charity.

Besides fixing and giving, the Elsens have done some going, too. John has travelled to Honduras several times on two-week Christian Medical Society projects. The couple also travelled to Africa with their pastor to visit missionaries.

"Sure there have been some problems and conflicts, and lots of work to it all. But when you add it all up, the pluses far outweigh the minuses," John says. "There's always great joy in doing the Lord's work. Plus we get all the friendships and experiences. I hesitate to use the word *fun*—it has such a superficial connotation—but that's what it has been. Fun."

The Elsens don't know how many people have stayed in their home and apartment. They're not sure how many cars they've given away. They just know they're doing what the Lord wants them to do.

Another shining example of a World Christian is John Maisal of Dallas. John is a born entrepreneur and has achieved success in a number of business ventures, including commercial real estate. Though a layman, he has the gift of evangelism. Leading men to Christ in his office is a regular part of a day's routine.

Besides serving on the missionary committee of the Fellowship Bible Church in Park City, he is a frequent speaker at missionary conferences in other churches. More recently he has organized tours to Eastern Europe, not to see the sights, but to give the tourists a glimpse of church life behind the Iron Curtain. After two or three tours, he was so deeply moved by the paucity of trained church leaders in that part of the world that he relinquished his business to give himself full time to promoting theological education. For two years now he has been the U.S. director of the Eastern European Seminary in Vienna, though he himself has had no formal theological training! At present he is spending part of his time in Vienna and part in Dallas—promoting home and foreign missions.

Jesus said, "Where your treasure is there will your heart be also." That is certainly true of John Maisal. His treasure has long since been evangelism and missions, not fame or fortune; and he has finally decided to devote all his time and energy to the work dearest to his heart. Imagine what our evangelical churches would be like if all our members were like John Maisal!

10

Living as a World Christian

Christianity is a life to be lived, not just a creed to be believed, or an organization to be joined, or a ritual to be performed. These things are important in their place, but the ultimate test of our faith is how we live our daily lives in the midst of a world whose value system is basically inimical to the gospel we espouse.

In every age the Christian church is in danger of taking on the complexion of its non-Christian environment. The individual Christian is always in danger of lowering his standards and adopting the manners and mores of the world. We must constantly remember the words of Paul, "Don't let the world around you squeeze you into its own mold" (Rom 12:2, *Phillips*). The world has its accepted code of social behavior. It is set conveniently in the scale—not too high and not too low. Every member of society is expected to know what that code is, and conformity is demanded of all. If one falls below the standard, he will be punished. If he dare rise above it, he will be persecuted. That is what happened to Jesus. He said, "They hated Me without a cause" (Jn 15:25). He was too good for them. That's why they got rid of Him.

Today's Christian finds himself in the same bind. Society naturally prefers an honest man to a dishonest man, but it doesn't want a person to be *scrupulously* honest. The boss doesn't want the employee to tell a lie *to* him, but on occasion he may require that he tell a lie *for* him. Likewise with religion. A little is good form; in fact, in some communities, it is good for business. But don't be *too* religious. Don't carry your religion with you into the marketplace. They'll call you a fanatic.

So the World Christian who decides to take his faith seriously and live according to the teachings of Christ will find himself in a minority—even in the church. This is especially true if he insists on carrying his religion into everyday life. If he insists on living by the Sermon on the Mount, he will be regarded as a fanatic. That is the price he will have to pay for his allegiance to Jesus Christ. He cannot forget the words of the Master, "He that findeth his life shall lose it: and he that loseth his life for my sake shall find it" (Mt 10:39, KJV). This being so, there are certain things the World Christian will be willing to do in his devotion to Christ and his dedication to His service.

Broaden the Scope of His Prayer Life

It is probably correct to say that prayer, especially intercessory prayer, is the weakest link in the chain of the Christian life. We would sooner do anything than pray—teach, preach, work, witness, and serve. The reason is not far to seek. Prayer—real prayer—is hard work, and prayer for others is the hardest form of prayer. We all agree that prayer is the source of our power; but somehow we are not convinced that it is absolutely essential to the success of the Christian life. We have mottoes on our walls: "Much prayer, much power. Little prayer, little power. No prayer, no power." But somehow we continue to go our way, thinking that if we try hard enough we will achieve at least a measure of success on our own. After all, we have all kinds of resources in men, money, experience, and expertise.

One reason why we don't pray more is that our prayers tend to be too self-centered. We seldom get beyond the physical, material, and spiritual needs of our own family and congregation. Certainly these are legitimate concerns for prayer, but prayer in the early church went far beyond that. Paul was himself a man of prayer, and he encouraged his converts to become the same. He taught them to pray for three things: all saints (Eph 6:18), all men (1 Tim 2:1), and all things (Ph 4:6)—a comprehensive scope.

If a man from Mars were to visit one of our midweek prayer meetings and listen to the prayer requests as they are announced, and then listen to the prayers that follow, he would not get the impression that this group of 10 or 20 persons was a local expression of a worldwide community whose interests and responsibilities extend to the ends of the earth. Frequently, not a single request or prayer goes beyond the narrow confines of the congregation.

The prayer list is often a long one. Johnnie fell out of a tree and broke his hip and is in the hospital. Mary is home from school with measles. Deacon Conrad lost his job and is looking for employment. Elder Johnson was involved in an accident and totaled his car. The Slater family welcomed a new baby last week. Patricia Baker leaves tomorrow for college. The summer offerings are down and the treasurer can't pay the bills. The pastor and his family are on vacation. The litany goes on and on. Strangely enough, everyone goes home happy, thinking the prayer meeting was a success!

But was it? No mention was made of the Billy Graham Crusade in Taiwan, or the earthquake in Guatemala, or the tidal wave in Bangladesh, or the famine in Uganda, or the American hostages in Iran, or the practice of genocide in Cambodia, or the loss of two MAF planes in Irian Jaya, or the persecution of the Christians in Cuba, or the turmoil in Poland, or the Soviet Union's invasion of Afghanistan, or a crucial election coming up in Indonesia, or the evacuation of missionaries from Vietnam. These and dozens of other crucial issues are never mentioned. And nobody noticed!

How different it was in the early church! Paul wrote to Timothy: "First of all, then, I urge that entreaties and prayers, petitions and thanksgivings, be made on behalf of all men, for kings and all who are in authority, in order that we may lead a tranquil and quiet life in all godliness and dignity. This is good and acceptable in the sight of God our Savior" (1 Tim 2:1–3).

When was the last time you prayed for the president of the United States? You might reply, "How can I pray for him? He's Republican and I'm a Democrat." Well, if he's a Republican that may be all the more reason you should pray for him! If that doesn't solve your problem, you *could* change parties! But all joking aside, when did you last pray for the president? Have you *ever* prayed for the Secretary General of the United Nations? Or the president of the World Bank? Or the members of the Supreme Court?

Are you concerned that the explosive situation in the Middle East might easily lead to World War III? If so, have you ever prayed for King Hussein of Jordan? If lasting peace ever comes to that part of the world he will doubtless play a major role.

Perhaps you don't believe that Christians should pray for such things. Not far from where I used to live in Northbrook, Illinois, there was a large outdoor poster with the words: "Get us out of the United Nations." What good would that do? The United Nations has not been as successful as its founders envisaged, but it has been more successful than its opponents give it credit for. It has prevented a number of wars and managed to restrict others. Besides, it is the one forum where world leaders of differing economic and political systems can sit down together and talk. Talking is better than shooting. And let us remember that Jesus said, "Blessed are the peacemakers, for they shall be called sons of God" (Mt 5:9). I have to believe that Jesus is on the side of peace and therefore looks with favor on every effort to achieve or maintain peace. For this reason I want the United Nations to succeed in its peacekeeping role and in its many other roles as well.

E. M. Bounds, in *Prayer,* has this to say: "It must never be forgotten that Almighty God rules this world. . . . He rules the world just as He rules the Church—by prayer." This is something that we Christians tend to forget. Indeed, some of us do not believe that He rules the world. The world, for some, has long since been taken over by Satan. He is its god and prince, and no good thing can ever come out of the world.

The World Christian will not subscribe to this notion for a moment. He believes with all his heart that the world, in spite of all its corruption and violence, is God's world and that He has a plan for the world as well as for the church. He is convinced that Christians are the salt of the earth and the light of the world. So, he believes, and the least he can do is to pray for the world leaders in their onerous task of keeping the peace.

Shortly before Shanghai fell to the Chinese Communists in 1949 the city was in turmoil. Students were demonstrating on the campuses; labor unions were threatening to go on strike; refugees from the north were wall-to-wall on the streets, with scores of them dying of malnutrition and exposure every night. At the height of the trouble, Bishop Frank Houghton, general director of the China Inland Mission (now the Overseas Missionary Fellowship) visited the mayor in his office. After exchanging the usual pleasantries, the mayor said to the bishop, "Well, what can I do for you?" Bishop Houghton replied, "I have no requests to make, your honor. I have come today to have prayer with you." The startled mayor blinked, gulped, and blurted out, "Go right ahead. I surely need all the help I can get." The bishop prayed for the city, the country, the economy, the war, the refugees; and then for the mayor that God would give him the wisdom, strength, and courage necessary to meet the demands of the hour.

When the bishop got up to leave the mayor said, "Thank you for coming. I appreciate your support and concern." Then he paused and added, "You know, there are 1,200 Christian missionaries in this city. You're the first one who ever came to pray with me!" What a sad comment. Even missionaries can miss the mark!

If it is true that God rules the world in answer to the prayers of His people, we had better get moving; for the days are evil; the time is short; and it is later than we think.

The World Christian will do his best praying in the evening, after he has heard the six o'clock news or had time to read the newspaper. And when he prays he will remember Pope John Paul II in Central America, the Secretary of State in China, Deng Xiaoping in Washington, the war in the Falkland Islands, the famine in Ethiopia, the refugees in Bangladesh, the unemployed in this country, the blacks, Hispanics, and other minorities in the ghettos of our big cities. And, of course, he will not forget the work and witness of the church at home or the life and labors of the missionaries in all parts of the world. In a word, he will embrace in his prayers both the church and the world, knowing that both belong to God and are therefore areas of legitimate concern. Finally, he will close with the majestic words of the Lord's Prayer: "Thy will be done on earth as it is in heaven."

It is easy to *talk* about praying; it is another to get down to the business of praying. Happily in this day we have ample resources to enable us to pray intelligently and specifically for the situation in every country in the world. One such resource is *Operation World: A Handbook for World Intercession,* by Patrick J. Johnstone, International Research Secretary of Worldwide Evangelization Crusade in England. This work appeared first in 1978 and has been revised several times since, so that it is always up to date. It may be purchased for a few dollars from the William Carey Library, P. O. Box 40129, Pasadena, California 91104.

The book covers 190 countries and territories in all six continents. Each country is given separate and detailed treatment. The section on each country is divided into two parts: Background and Points for Prayer. Under part 1, information is provided on area, population, peoples, capital, economy, politics, and religion. The material in this part is factual, detailed, comprehensive, remarkably accurate and up to date.

The second part includes points for prayer. Here the coverage depends on the size of the country and the amount of Christian and missionary work there. For Macao, for instance, there are only 2 items for prayer. For India, on the other hand, 31 prayer items are listed and they take up four pages.

In addition to information about the individual countries, there are 12 pages devoted to an introduction to the world. There are also introductions to the various regions of the world—Asia, Africa, Latin America. These are extremely helpful in giving the reader a bird's-eye view of the overall religious situation in these regions. I cannot speak too highly of this book. I heartily recommend it to every World Christian who desires to pray seriously on a regular basis, for church and mission, at home as well as abroad. I personally use the book every morning in my devotions. I would not be without it.

Adopt a Simple Lifestyle

If I were an artist I would paint a picture in two parts. On the right I would have a large round table with three place settings—one for the father and one each for a son and a daughter. On this table I would place all kinds of good things to eat—meat, fish, fowl, cabbage, beans, broccoli, carrots, and cauliflower. I would have various kinds of potato—fried, baked, and mashed. For dessert I would have a choice of pastry, pie or ice cream, or an assortment of fruit—peaches, pears, oranges, and bananas. For a beverage the two children could have Coke, Sprite, Orange Crush, or Mountain Dew; the father could have tea, coffee, or cocoa.

On the other side of my picture I would have another table, with nine place settings, one for the mother and one each for the eight children. At each place setting I would have a glass of water, a bowl of soup, and a crust of bread.

And I would call my work of art "The American Family at Dinner." You would come along, inspect my picture, read the caption, and shake your head, saying, "No! No! That's a lie. From Maine to California there isn't a single family in which that kind of wealth and that kind of poverty can be found. We have rich families and they share their riches. We have poor families and they share their poverty; but no matter where you look you won't find a single family that combines that kind of wealth and that kind of poverty. That picture is a lie."

And you would be right! The picture *is* a lie. But suppose I were to change the title and call my work of art "The Human Family at Dinner." I should be precisely on the mark. That is how the human family lives—part in poverty that beggars description and part in wealth that borders on the obscene.

Economically, the world is divided into two parts—the "have" nations and the "have not" nations. The gap between the two is getting bigger with every passing year. In fact, it is so great that it is difficult to take it in unless the situation is placed in perspective by reducing it to a microcosm. I have in my file such a scenario and I give it here.

If we could compress the total population of the world, which now stands at 4.8 billion persons, into a community of 1,000 persons living in a single town, the following picture of contrasts would emerge: 60 persons would represent the population of the United States; the remainder of the world would be represented by 940 persons. The 60 Americans would be receiving half the total income of the entire community; the other 940 persons would have to share the remaining half.

The 60 Americans would have 15 times as many possessions per person as the others, and would consume 12 times as much electric power, 22 times more coal, 21 times more oil and gasoline, 50 times as much steel, and 50 times as much in general equipment of all kinds.

The 60 Americans, moreover, would have an average life span of more than 70 years; all the others would average about 40 years.

Most of the 940 non-Americans in the community would always be hungry, most of them poor, ignorant, illiterate, and sick. Half of them would be unable to read or write. Half of them would never have heard of Jesus Christ.

The picture may be an oversimplification, but the main thrust is clear. The "have" nations have too much and people in the "have not" nations go to bed hungry every night. The "have" nations are exhausting the resources of science to find a cheap and easy way to remove the calories from our food while the "have not" nations are crying out for more food, more fat, more protein, more and more calories. I often wonder what God thinks about the situation. I'm sure He cannot be pleased. Certainly the grinding poverty of the Third World is not His doing. We, in the West, must bear much of the responsibility.

Someone may wish to challenge these facts and point out that we have our own problems with poverty and unemployment in the ghettos of our large cities, and hold that we should address them first and think of the rest of the world later. It is true, we have "pockets of poverty" in the ghettos of our large cities and in depressed regions like Appalachia, and we should be doing all we can to cope with the problem. But in the Third World, poverty is well-nigh universal. For three billion people it is a way of life from which there is no escape. The poverty here is nothing compared with the poverty there. Our poor have food stamps, Medicaid, Aid to Dependent Children. Many drive their own cars and have running water and electricity in their homes. Jim Wallis, of the Sojourners, in Washington, D.C., has this to say:

> I will never forget the first time I visited a shanty town on the outskirts of the Third World city. People lived in makeshift shelters made of discarded metal and wood

scraps, tar paper, and cardboard. There was no sanitation, no running water, no electricity, and little food. Women hauled unclean water from two miles away. I didn't have to ask what kind of education the children were getting. Disease, illiteracy, high infant mortality, and, of course, hunger were the daily experience of the people. In the worst sections of Detroit, Chicago, and the District of Columbia, or the South Bronx, I have never seen such human misery.[1]

The World Christian can't be satisfied with the status quo. He will want to go back to the Bible to see what God has to say about the problems of poverty, and he will be surprised to find the prominence given to the subject. After studying what Scripture has to say on the subject, Wallis said:

It pervades the Old Testament and . . . is the second most common topic found there, the first being idolatry. . . . In the New Testament we found more than 500 verses of direct teaching on the subject . . . Jesus talked more about wealth and poverty than almost any other subject, including heaven and hell, sexual morality, the law, or violence. One out of every ten verses in the Synoptic Gospels is about the rich and the poor; in Luke the ratio is one out of seven.[2]

Obedience to Scripture will force the World Christian to bring his whole value system under review. He will remember that poverty was at the heart of the Incarnation, when He who was rich for our sakes became poor, that we *through His poverty* might be rich (2 Cor 8:9).

Jesus was the only person who, before He came into the world, had the authority to select His own circumstances. Yet He deliberately by-passed the homes of the high, the powerful, and the rich, and chose to be born into a poor and humble home in the despised town of Nazareth. The World Christian will remember the warning of Jesus to His disciples, that a man's life does not consist in the abundance of

1. Jim Wallis, *The Call to Conversion: Recovering the Gospel for These Times* (New York: Harper and Row, 1981), pp. 43–44.
2. Ibid., pp. 57–58.

things that he possesses (Lk 12:15). He will also remember what Jesus said about the folly of laying up treasures on earth (Mt 6:19). He will take to heart the question raised by Jesus: "What does it profit a man to gain the whole world, and forfeit his soul?" (Mk 8:36).

A study of Scripture will convince the World Christian that while God has no favorites, He is definitely on the side of the poor, precisely because their poverty is often caused by the oppression of the rich and powerful.

No one individual may be able to alter the power structures of American society, but the World Christian will want to do what he can—beginning with himself. He will make a deliberate decision to simplify his own lifestyle so that he might have more of this world's goods to share with the poor, especially the poor of the Third World. He will agree with John Wesley in his philosophy of wealth: "Make all you can. Save all you can. Give away all you can." And Wesley practiced what he preached. In his early years his annual income was 30 pounds. He lived on 27 and gave the rest away. Some years later when his income doubled to 60 pounds a year, he continued to live on 27 and gave the rest away. When his income climbed to 90 pounds a year, he still lived on 27.

Simplifying one's lifestyle is not easy, for two reasons. First, we have enjoyed our affluence so long we have come to take it for granted. We assume we have a right to it. Besides, everyone around us is doing the same. It takes a good deal of courage in American society deliberately to adopt a simple lifestyle, especially when a wife and children may be involved. The neighbors won't understand; and the children may have a hard time.

I pass on to you something which startled me when I first read it. The title was: "You can live on $100 a year. Millions do. Here's how."

Get rid of all your furniture except one table, and one chair. Throw out your lamps, TV, radio and stereo. Dispose of all your clothing except a couple of dresses or one suit. Keep one pair of shoes for the head of the family.

Shut off the water, gas, and electricity, and get rid of the car. Give away all your kitchen appliances and move the family to the tool-shed. Keep a small bag of flour, some sugar and salt, a few potatoes, a handful of onions and some dried beans.

Forget about newspapers, magazines, and books. Count your emergency fund at about $5.00. No bankbooks, no pension plans, no insurance policies. Pray fervently that you don't get sick.

Try to find three acres of land that you can cultivate as a tenant farmer. If there's no drought, expect $100–$300 for the year's cash crops. Pay one-third to the landlord, and another chunk to the moneylender.[3]

Nobody in his right mind would suggest that we can live on $100 a year. We couldn't live on $1,000 a year, or even $3,000. But many of us could cut our living expenses 10 or 20 percent a year and not really miss it. We could begin by cutting out the luxuries, and they alone might save us several thousand dollars a year. The only problem with this is that after living with the luxuries for a year or two they become necessities and thus hard to give up. But with resolve it can be done.

The World Christian will search for ways to simplify his lifestyle. He will ask himself some hard questions. *Must* I turn in my car every year or two? *Must* I remain in a large house after the children have gone to college? *Must* I buy a new suit of clothes simply because the lapels are a bit narrow? *Must* I take a winter vacation in Florida as well as a summer vacation in the Adirondacks? If he is serious about the matter, the World Christian will *find* ways to simplify his lifestyle. And after a year or two he will discover that he is spending less but enjoying it more.

---

3. American Baptist Churches in the U.S.A.

There are several books that the World Christian will find helpful at this point. I mention only five: *The Golden Cow* by John White, *Global Living Here and Now* by James A. Scherer, *Rich Christians in an Age of Hunger* by Ronald J. Sider, *The Call to Conversion* by Jim Wallis, and *The Mustard Seed Conspiracy* by Tom Sine. These books are radical yet realistic, probing yet practical, unsettling yet stimulating. They ought to be read carefully and prayerfully by every American who aspires to become a World Christian.

The World Christian who succeeds in simplifying his lifestyle will soon discover that he has not lost much. For as E. Stanley Jones was fond of saying: "There are two ways in which a person can be rich. One is in the multiplicity of his possessions and the other is in the simplicity of his wants." This is absolutely true. It is amazing what we can get along without and still be happy and productive. I know this from personal experience. When my wife and I had been in China less than three years we lost everything we possessed when our city was completely destroyed by the Japanese air force. Because of the war, it was impossible to replace our belongings; nevertheless we remained at our post for another six years, and barely missed the things we lost. It *is* possible to have less and enjoy it more.

For those who want to make a serious effort to simplify their lifestyle, Sider has a helpful chart (see Table 1). The basic 10 percent tithe applies to the first $10,000 of income. For each additional $1,000 of income, the tithe increases by 5 percent. The principle is a good one and merits consideration. There are many ways in which we as World Christians can do better than we have in the past.

Spend Some Time Overseas

I advocate that every American spend at least a year or two overseas before he gets married, settles down, and

Table 1*

Total income	Tithe: Per cent of additional thousand	Tithe: Per cent of the whole	Total given away	Personal expenditures and savings
10,000	–	10.0%	$ 1,000	$ 9,000
11,000	15%	10.5%	1,150	9,850
12,000	20%	11.3%	1,350	10,650
13,000	25%	12.3%	1,600	11,400
14,000	30%	13.6%	1,900	12,100
15,000	35%	15.0%	2,250	12,750
16,000	40%	16.6%	2,650	13,350
17,000	45%	18.2%	3,100	13,900
18,000	50%	20.0%	3,600	14,400
19,000	55%	21.8%	4,150	14,850
20,000	60%	23.8%	4,750	15,250
21,000	65%	25.7%	5,400	15,600
22,000	70%	27.7%	6,100	15,900
23,000	75%	29.8%	6,850	16,150
24,000	80%	31.9%	7,650	16,350
25,000	85%	34.0%	8,500	16,500
26,000	90%	36.2%	9,400	16,600
27,000	95%	38.3%	10,350	16,650
28,000	100%	40.5%	11,350	16,650

*Taken from *Rich Christians in an Age of Hunger: Revised and Expanded* by Ronald J. Sider. Second edition © 1984 by Inter-Varsity Christian Fellowship of the USA and used by permission of InterVarsity Press, Downers Grove, IL 60515.

raises a family. When he returns he will be a better, more intelligent citizen. He will have an appreciation for the people and problems of the Third World that most Americans now simply do not have and will never acquire. He will listen to the six o'clock news and read the morning newspaper with keener interest and deeper understanding. He will no longer espouse the notion *my country right or wrong*. He will have a clearer picture of world affairs and a better understanding of their complexity. The years he spends abroad may well turn out to be the most significant years of his life.

If this is true of the average American, how much more is it true of the person who aspires to be a World Christian? He has an incentive that no purely secular purpose can provide. His Master is the Lord of history and is working out His plans and purposes on a global scale. It is His intention to save the world, and He has His workers in all parts of the world, building His kingdom on earth. The World Christian will want to be identified with the ongoing purposes of God for the church and for the world.

If his stay abroad is to be worthwhile he must not stop in London, or Paris, or Rome. He must keep going at least until he reaches the Suez Canal. There he will discover for the very first time what it means to be a "foreigner." *Everything* will be strange—the food, the clothes, the climate, the culture, the language, and the religion. Now he is beginning to *see the world*!

Living overseas, even for a short time, will do several things for him.

First, it will enable him to see how the "other half" of the world lives. He has probably had glimpses on television, but that is a far cry from being there in person. Famine is little more than a word in the dictionary until one has seen India after a monsoon failure. All my life I have seen pictures of the Grand Canyon, but it wasn't until last summer that I stood on the north rim of the canyon and, with a dizzy head and a tingling spine, I leaned over and looked down at the Colorado River 6,000 feet below. So it is with famine, hunger, and disease. These things must be seen to be comprehended.

Second, he will see the people, mostly poor, hard-working peasants—hundreds of millions of them. He will note their indomitable spirit, their will to live, their willingness to share, their quiet sense of humor, their incredible patience under oppression, their dignity in the face of disaster, and their contentment with the simple things of life.

Third, he will see the Christian church in an entirely unfamiliar setting—a small, struggling, often persecuted minority surrounded by a mass of non-Christian humanity. He will see rural churches without buildings, budgets, Bibles, or hymnbooks, yet showing amazing vitality and growth. He will learn what it means for a lone Christian to be a light shining in a dark place—a Christian man unable to find employment, a Christian woman unable to find a believing husband, Christian children enduring ridicule in the public school. He will see faithful, hard-working, inadequately trained pastors with large families, small churches, and plenty of problems. He will note the simplicity of their faith, the warmth of their love, the depth of their dedication, and their willingness to endure hardship for the sake of the gospel.

When he returns, the World Christian will never be the same again. He will be a better husband, father, deacon, Sunday-school teacher, youth leader, church worker, and missionary-committee member. In a word, he will be a better Christian, and to his dying day he will recall the familiar sights and sounds of the church at work, worship, and witness in a predominantly non-Christian environment. And he will give thanks to God for the power of the gospel, for the work of missions, and for the strength of the church in the Third World.

But the World Christian will not be content with a year or two overseas. He may want to live abroad for an indefinite period. Fifty years ago such opportunities were few and far between. Today they abound. According to the *U.S.*

News and World Report, there were 1.5 million United States private citizens living abroad in 1979. The figure is higher today. They are found in practically every country of the world and are engaged in a wide range of occupations.

The term *tentmaker* is borrowed from the apostle Paul, who made tents to pay expenses. How is the term used today? Strictly speaking a tentmaker is a dedicated Christian who lives and works overseas, under nonreligious auspices, *for the express purpose* of using his secular calling as an opportunity to give his witness to Jesus Christ.

It should be noted that the *intent* is important. Not every Christian working overseas is a tentmaker. A young executive with IBM who is transferred to Tokyo may be a dedicated Christian, but his *express purpose* in going to Tokyo is not to spread the faith. He is simply accepting a transfer with a corresponding increment in salary. Such a person should not be called a tentmaker. He is an ordinary businessman on the way up the executive ladder, and will probably be back in the United States before long. His *motive* in going to Tokyo is to advance his business career, not to share the gospel. Hence he should not be considered a tentmaker in the strict sense of the term.

The American or British tentmaker has one big advantage. His native tongue is the lingua franca of the contemporary world. According to a recent report in *Newsweek,* English, understood by 750 million people, is the most widely spoken language in the world. Though more people speak Chinese, they are concentrated largely in one country. In the rest of the world, Chinese is practically unknown except by overseas Chinese. It is thus possible for an English-speaking tentmaker today to go to almost any large city in the world and be understood. Indeed, English is in such demand around the world that if missionaries wanted to, they could spend all their time teaching English.

Another advantage is that the tentmaker is welcome in countries closed to the professional missionary. Most Muslim and Communist countries are in this category, including the People's Republic of China. With more and more countries refusing to accept missionaries, this may be our only way of carrying out the Great Commission in the twenty-first century. Centainly it is one of the exciting possibilities of the future and one for which the church should be prepared. We should begin by recognizing these tentmakers as bona fide missionaries, place them on our prayer list, and give them all the moral support they deserve.

One is not necessarily forced to choose between being a tentmaker and a professional missionary. It is possible to be a full member of a mission, with all the rights and privileges attached thereto, and at the same time hold a teaching position in a government school or a secular university. In Nigeria there is a strong demand for qualified teachers to teach Religious Knowledge in the high schools. Such teachers are full faculty members and paid by the government; at the same time they are members of the Sudan Interior Mission. The same is true of a score of tentmakers with the Overseas Missionary Fellowship in Asia. One of them prepared the curriculum for the study of Christianity to be used in all government schools in Indonesia. There is nothing secret about this. The facts are known by the governments concerned. They have no objections to having Christians teach in their universities. In some instances, they prefer them.

Some countries are completely closed to professional missionaries, but open to tentmakers; among them are China, Saudi Arabia, and Afghanistan. In all such countries the tentmakers must walk a tightrope. One false move, one unwise word, and out they go. In China they are under close surveillance and are not permitted to establish friendly relations with the people. Under such conditions, opportunities for a verbal witness are almost nil. Nevertheless, the tentmakers who are there now—and I know some of them—consider it a high privilege to be in China under any conditions. To be in a non-Christian country the size of China and not be able to do the very thing you went there to do is extremely frustrating. They surely need our prayers.

Many of the so-called faith missions now accept tentmakers as full or associate members. Some agencies, such as Campus Crusade for Christ, Navigators, Inter-Varsity Christian Fellowship, Operation Mobilization, Youth With A Mission, and others encourage American students to take a year or two off and study in a university overseas. Universities the world over are open to foreign nationals. Indeed, some of them are delighted to have Western students in the classroom.

Another form of ministry is open to the World Christian. It occurs at the upper end of the age spectrum—55 and over. An increasing number of Christians are going overseas after they retire. Indeed, some of them retire early in order to have 10 or 15 good years on the mission field. They are known as second careerists. With Social Security and a pension or two, these people are usually financially independent, which makes them doubly welcome to the mission boards. They are older, more mature, more dependable than youth and as such can function very effectively in a number of capacities on the mission field, without ever becoming a full-fledged missionary of the conventional sort. Some grandparents have been known to visit their children and grandchildren on the field, only to find such a warm welcome and so many things to do that they stay on for a year or two before coming home. Teachers who have taught for 40 years at home can certainly teach overseas. They are especially welcome in schools for missionaries' children. Others can serve as hosts and hostesses in mission homes. Still others have been known to catalog books, manage bookstores, repair broken furniture and equipment, do office work and a hundred-and-one other chores that need to be done. It is an exciting and profitable way to end the Christian life—in harness on the mission field.

Of course, there is always the chance that a person might die overseas. So what? The distance to heaven from

New Delhi is no greater than from New York. And there is one fringe benefit—funeral expenses are only a fraction of what they are at home!

In tentmaking missionary work, as in so many other things, there are advantages and disadvantages. The reader may find chapter 8 in my *Winds of Change in the Christian Mission* helpful. Also, I would strongly recommend *Today's Tentmakers* by J. Christy Wilson, Jr. Its 20 chapters are packed with information, not found elsewhere, that will help you make up your mind about becoming a tentmaker.

PART 4

A Summary
The Future of World Missions

11

World Missions in the Twenty-first Century

In another 15 years we will enter the twenty-first century. What will it mean to the Christian church and to world missions?

Will we be able to consolidate the gains of the twentieth century and go on to even bigger and better things in the future? Will the present interest in world missions continue? If so, will we be able to convert the interest into action? If doors continue to close will the professional missionary become a vanishing breed? At the rate we are going, is there any hope of completing the task of world evangelization in the foreseeable future?

At the start of the twentieth century the slogan was, "The evangelization of the world in this generation." After a hundred years of arduous toil and many setbacks we have a better understanding of the magnitude of the task; consequently we have dropped the slogan as too optimistic and too simplistic. We have concluded that the task is unattainable. But is it?

Can the World Be Won?

The answer is yes, and no, depending on one's point of view. If we continue to employ the halfhearted, ill-conceived, poorly-executed methods of the past, the answer is no. But if we can mobilize the entire Christian community to the point where every church member becomes a World Christian and every church becomes a witnessing community, there is no telling what could be accomplished in the century ahead.

If every church took its divinely-given responsibility seriously and devoted to the task of world evangelization all the resources at its command, we might be surprised by the results. If every evangelical Christian were to become a World Christian, the manpower problem, for one thing, would be solved in short order. We would have all the candidates required to finish the job and we would have all the funds necessary to train them, equip them, send them out, and fully support them indefinitely on the mission fields of the world.

Almost two thousand years ago Christ commissioned His disciples to "make disciples of all nations." The early church took the Great Commission seriously, and its members, in a matter of weeks, were accused of filling Jerusalem with the doctrine. And from Jerusalem it spread through Judea to Samaria and from there to the ends of the then-known world; so that after one generation Paul could state that the eastern half of the empire had been evangelized, and he was turning his face toward Spain (Rom 15:17–24). Alas, subsequent generations did not do as well. The Protestant churches in Europe, for instance, for two hundred years were content to evangelize the "heathen" in Europe while the rest of the world—Asia, Africa, and the New World—was woefully neglected.

Significant progress has been made in the last two hundred years, but in recent decades world population has soared so rapidly that the number of non-Christians in the world is many times greater than when William Carey went to India in 1793. Indeed, there are today more non-Christians in India and China than there are Christians in the entire world!

As long as the Christian church continues to regard world missions as one of the last and least of its responsibilities, and devotes only a tiny fraction of its total resources in men and money to the cause of Christ around the world, the task will never be completed. As it is, most of the churches in the Western world are self-centered, inward-looking, preaching self-denial but all the while practicing self-indulgence. They are preoccupied with their own problems and concerned almost exclusively for their own growth. They are playing at missions.

The Tragedy of a False Dichotomy

Looking back, we now know that we made a serious mistake in the past. We settled for an unfortunate dichotomy in the church. A few brave, noble, dedicated souls with a sense of "call" became missionaries. Somehow, these people were always a bit "strange"—a breed apart. By the world they were regarded as religious zealots. By the church they were admired but not emulated, applauded but not taken very seriously.

Their strength lay in the fact that they were completely sold out to Jesus Christ. Like the early Christians, they understood the meaning of discipleship; they took their cue from Christ who was their Lord and Master as well as their Friend and Savior. Consequently they did some "strange" things: They helped the poor. They healed the sick. They cleansed the leper. They educated the illiterate. They liked foreigners. They welcomed strangers. They even loved their enemies. They did everything but raise the dead! They were saints and only saints could be missionaries. At least, that is what we thought.

It was all or nothing. One was either a full-fledged, full-time career missionary or one was a comfortable, respectable, self-satisfied church member with no *direct, personal* responsibility for the evangelization of the world. If the "call" came, you went; if it didn't, you were free to stay at

home and do your own thing. The number of people getting
the "call" was always a tiny fraction of the total membership of any congregation. Indeed, thousands of
churches never produced a single missionary. That made
the missionary all the more "special."

The people with the "call" were regarded as especially
spiritual and were expected to live a life of faith (which
meant living from hand to mouth), enduring loneliness,
privation, misunderstanding, and rejection. The people
without the "call" were free to go their own way, get good
jobs, raise fine families, live in beautiful homes in the
luxury and security of suburbia. Those with the "call"
were expected to make all the sacrifices while the others
were free to enjoy the good things of life bestowed on them
by a kind and generous heavenly Father.

This unwarranted, unbiblical dichotomy has been di-
sastrous, both for the cause of missions overseas and for
the health and well-being of the church at home. It has
involved the missionary in unnecessary hardship and privation. At the same time, it has robbed the church of spiritual enrichment. It was a mistake that such a dichotomy
ever began. It is a major misfortune that it has been perpetuated so long.

Total Mobilization

If the world is ever to be evangelized, in this generation
or any other, this dichotomy must somehow be broken.
Those who remain at home must realize that they too are
intimately and personally involved in world missions even
though they are not missionaries in the technical sense of
the word. Their chief concern will not be for their own
advancement or enrichment, or that of their family, but
the evangelization of the world. They, as well as the missionaries, must learn to seek first the kingdom of God and
His righteousness. Pastors and other church leaders will
have to recognize that their chief concern is not bigger

budgets and better buildings, or even more programs and more people, but a deeper commitment to the cause of Christ on a global scale.

The idea is catching on. A new agency, "Caleb Project," is taking the lead and sending new recruits from a dozen cooperating missions to churches and colleges all over the country, with exciting results.

If the Acts of the Apostles is anything to go by, the early church was indeed a witnessing community. The two key words in the Book of Acts are found in Acts 1:8. They are "witness" and "power." Throughout the entire book these two ideas run deep. Luke is concerned only with those events that contributed, directly or indirectly, to the spread of the gospel and the expansion of the church. Some of the churches were started by the apostles, especially the apostle Paul; others were started by lay persons, some of them refugees and other displaced persons. Luke tells us that when the Christians in Jerusalem were persecuted after the death of Stephen, the disciples "went about preaching the Word" (Acts 8:4). The famous church in Antioch was started by just such a group (Acts 11:19).

It was also true of the Moravians in the eighteenth century. Their colony, known as Herrnhut in Saxony, became the nerve center of a worldwide network of missionary activity. Its members, single and married, were prepared to go to the ends of the earth at the drop of a hat. Whenever a call came, they drew lots and the one or ones on whom the lot fell left as soon as possible for some remote part of the earth.

Those who remained at Herrnhut were as much a part of the missionary outreach as those who went abroad. And they organized a prayer vigil that lasted for a hundred years! The first two missionaries to Greenland were gravediggers. Of the first two missionaries to the West Indies, one was a potter and the other one a carpenter. When a man named Sorensen was asked if he were ready to go to Labrador, he replied, "Yes, tomorrow, if I am only given a pair of shoes." With such an attitude, little wonder that the Moravian Church was the greatest missionary agency of the eighteenth century.

The secret of their success lay in the fact that they were firmly convinced that world missions is the supreme task of the church, and that the responsibility for carrying out that task rests with every member of the Christian community, not just the leaders.

This being so, we are encouraged to believe that it can be done again. In more recent times the Christian and Missionary Alliance has come as close as anyone to achieving this ideal. After one hundred years the C&MA is still predominantly a *missionary* organization, and under the leadership of Louis King it intends to remain that way. If other denominations in the Western world had the spiritual vitality and the missionary vision of the C&MA, our prospects of success would be much greater.

The Increasing Role of the Laity

In the past there has been a sharp distinction in the church between the clergy and the laity, between the missionary and the nonmissionary. Today that distinction is breaking down. Even in the Roman Catholic Church lay people are taking an increasingly active part in the service of the church. In Protestant circles we have come a long way. Lay persons, women as well as men, are participating in the Sunday morning worship service to the enrichment of all.

Who knows? We may be entering a new era when missionary work will not be left to professional missionaries, but will be the common task of the rank and file of church members in the course of their daily occupations. It is encouraging to see the large number of people who want to go to China as tentmakers. They'll do anything to get into China! Some are in the diplomatic corps. Others are in the employ of a large corporation. Still others are teaching

English in colleges and universities all over China—and they are paying their own way to do it!

Hundreds of dedicated college students spend the summer in Beijing and Shanghai just studying the Chinese language; they are drawn there not simply by the lure of China's rich and ancient culture, but by the hope, however slim, that they might have an opportunity to share their faith with the intellectually starved students of China.

There are indications that a groundswell may be developing along these lines. The dichotomy between missionary and nonmissionary seems to be breaking down, and lay persons in all walks of life are making an unprecedented attempt to get involved in world evangelization. They want to know how their talents and expertise can be used in the service of Christ overseas. Thousands go abroad every summer. Other thousands are engaged in short-term missionary service, and not a few of them end up as career missionaries.

This trend should by all means be encouraged. Not only young people but also middle-aged people and senior citizens should be encouraged to get involved in various kinds of Christian service at home and overseas. Whether one goes abroad or remains at home does not matter. With jet travel—fast, convenient, and economical—there is no reason for anyone to hesitate to spend a summer overseas. All dedicated Christians should be prepared, like Sorensen at Herrnhut, to answer the call of need and be willing to go where the Spirit leads and circumstances permit.

In increasing numbers, people are getting the idea that they *can* make a contribution to world missions without ever becoming a missionary. In recent years, thousands of Christian tourists have visited China, taking Bibles with them. Indeed, some of them went for that express purpose and have been back several times. While 1.8 million copies of the Scriptures have been published in China in the last four years, an equal number of Bibles has been taken in by tourists, not to mention the Bibles that have been "smuggled" in by various organizations specializing in that kind of operation.

Many denominations, and some faith missions, now have programs designed to encourage lay persons to donate a month or more of their time to Christian work overseas. Such projects include construction, rehabilitation, community development, or disaster relief. It is not uncommon for a group of 20 or 30 persons to devote their summer vacation to helping the national churches in the Third World. And they return home with the satisfaction of having done a solid piece of work to which they can always look back with a sense of pride and satisfaction.

Some specialized agencies are devoted entirely to this kind of operation. One of them is Project Partner in Middletown, Ohio. Several times each year the mission organizes a work team of 20 to 30 people, old and young, men and women, who spend four to six weeks in Latin America. In the past 15 years five thousand people have participated in overseas projects; some five hundred of these people have become career missionaries or are now serving as pastors here at home. Altogether, they have helped build more than five hundred churches, medical clinics, and schools in 22 countries.

Several Mennonite groups, working through the Mennonite Central Committee, have for years engaged in this type of lay ministry all over the world. The first group of Paxmen went to Europe in 1951 to serve for two or three years in the refugee camps. Since then well over a thousand Paxmen have served in Asia, Africa, Latin America, and the Middle East. They work in such diverse fields as agriculture, mechanics, construction, maintenance, radio, education, relief, and office work. Beginning in 1962, the MCC introduced a second program for teachers only, known as Teachers Abroad Program. Working almost exclusively in Africa, TAP has placed hundreds of teachers in strategic short-term positions. In 1984 the Southern Baptist Convention had 6,213 short-term (one to four months) Volunteers, in addition to 211 Journeymen (two years), serving overseas.

Another promising development is the Christian medical clinic owned and operated by several dedicated doctors. Each year one of the doctors serves overseas, supported by the proceeds of the clinic. Neither church nor mission is involved in any additional expense. Moreover, it gives the doctor and his family firsthand contact with Christian missions and a personal exposure to another culture. It also greatly enhances the education of the children. The entire family returns home with a warm feeling of having enriched themselves while helping others. The following year another doctor and his family repeat the performance.

The Role of the Holy Spirit

If we are to make any headway in the evangelization of the world with almost five billion human beings, we shall need to give greater recognition to the person and power of the Holy Spirit.

It is fair to say that the Holy Spirit is the most ignored person of the Holy Trinity. This is seen in our hymns, our prayers, our preaching, and our writing. For every book on the Holy Spirit there are scores on the life of Christ. The average hymnal does well to have only a few hymns relating to the Holy Spirit. And even when our sermons deal with the Holy Spirit, the emphasis is more often on His person, not His power; His attributes, not His actions.

This is all the more strange when we remember that the present dispensation—from Pentecost to the Second Coming—is *the* dispensation of the Holy Spirit. While Christ is the Head of the church, the Holy Spirit is the Executive Director of the church's life and ministry. Just as no one can come to the Father except through Christ (Jn. 14:6), so no one can come to Christ except through the Holy Spirit (1 Cor 12:3).

This comes out clearly in the Acts of the Apostles where the Holy Spirit is mentioned more than 50 times. In chapter 1, He is the Spirit of promise. In chapter 2, He is the Spirit of utterance. In chapter 3, He is the Spirit of healing. In chapter 4, He is the Spirit of boldness. In chapter 5, He is the Spirit of holiness. In chapter 6, He is the Spirit of wisdom. In chapter 7, He is the Spirit of glory. In chapter 8, He is the Spirit of evangelism. In chapter 9, He is the Spirit of comfort. In chapter 10, He is the Spirit of guidance. And so on throughout the entire book. And Paul's parting words in chapter 28 refer to the Holy Spirit who spoke through Isaiah the prophet.

We have paid attention to the "go" in the Great Commission, but we have all but ignored the warning to "tarry" in Jerusalem until endued with power from on high. The warning referred, of course, to the historic event of Pentecost, which was a once-for-all event; but is there not implicit in this warning a reminder of the solemn fact that the world mission of the Christian church is a supernatural operation, calling for supernatural power?

At least that is the way the leading missionary statesmen of another day saw the situation. Robert H. Glover wrote, "Christian missions are no human undertaking, but a supernatural and divine enterprise for which God has provided supernatural power and leadership."[1] In another place he wrote, "He [the Holy Spirit] came as the divine Commander-in-chief of the forces and the campaign, and was at once recognized and acknowledged as such. His coming imparted the divine character to every aspect of the enterprise."[2]

The same note was sounded by John R. Mott: "Missionaries . . . are absolutely united in the conviction that world evangelization is a divine enterprise, that the Spirit of God is the great missioner, and that only as He domi-

---

1. Robert H. Glover, *The Bible Basis of Missions* (Chicago: Moody, 1964), p. 70.
2. Ibid., p. 63.

nates the work and workers can we hope for success in the undertaking to carry the knowledge of Christ to all people."[3]

Too long have we neglected to recognize the crucial role of the Holy Spirit in the life of the church. Someone has said that if the Holy Spirit were to be withdrawn from the world today, 90 percent of the churches would carry on next Sunday, business as usual, without even being aware that He had taken His leave. John E. Skoglund in *To the Whole Creation* has a chapter on the role of the Holy Spirit in world missions. He calls the chapter "The Missing Person." That is precisely what He is—the Missing Person.

If we are to make any impact on the world of the twenty-first century we must go back to the New Testament, especially the Acts of the Apostles, and discover how world missions were carried on by the early church. To the early Christians the Holy Spirit was a living, bright reality, and the entire ministry of the early church revolved around the Holy Spirit. His presence was recognized (Acts 15:28). His power was invoked (Acts 4:30). His directives were obeyed (Acts 13:2–3). His guidance was received (Acts 16:6–8). His administration was acknowledged (Acts 20:28).

In our own day we have ample evidence that the groups that emphasize the presence and power of the Holy Spirit are the ones that, year after year, are showing the greatest growth at home and overseas. And the growth is not simply quantitative; it is qualitative as well. Their converts last, their members witness, their leaders pray, their churches multiply. And they seem to get results where others labor with little or nothing to show for their efforts.

This comes through loud and clear in Patrick J. Johnstone's *Operation World*. He is obliged to acknowledge that in country after country the Pentecostals, in spite of their immense fragmentation, are the largest and fastest

---

3. John R. Mott, *The Decisive Hour of Christian Missions* (New York: Student Volunteer Movement, 1910), p. 103.

growing group. This is especially true in Latin America where they represent 70 percent of the Protestants. When writing about Finland, Johnstone remarks, "The Pentecostals are the strongest by far, and have enriched the spiritual life of the country, and are open to the strong charismatic movement within sections of the Lutheran Church."[4]

Writing about Costa Rica he makes the following statement: "Roman Catholic opposition to the gospel has waned, and in its place has risen a very evangelical charismatic movement. The evangelistic work of these charismatics has won more people to the Lord in 5 years than the Protestants in 50."[5]

We can thank God for the charismatic movement which has infiltrated nearly every denomination in the world. In most denominations the charismatic churches are the ones that are showing the greatest vision and vitality. They are growing in strength and numbers when other churches in the same denominations are struggling to maintain the status quo. Who knows? Maybe the charismatic movement is the Lord's last attempt to revive and renew His church so that she might become a thing of strength and beauty in the earth, and in the power of the Holy Spirit produce a great ingathering just before the Second Coming of Christ.

The Place for Signs and Wonders

Another encouraging sign is the number of evangelicals who are making a fresh study of "signs and wonders" as they relate to world evangelization.

It is a great pity that evangelicals in the United States have been divided on this rather controversial subject. Un-

---

4. Patrick J. Johnstone, *Operation World: A Handbook for World Intercession* (Bromley, England: STL Publications, 1980), p. 63.
5. Ibid., p. 282.

til recently, many evangelicals rejected signs and wonders; they did so on theological grounds. They believed that certain spiritual gifts in the early church were meant to be permanent and others were meant to be temporary. Among the latter were signs and wonders and the gift of tongues. The rationale for this interpretation was that once the canon was closed and Christianity was well established in the Roman Empire, the need for signs and wonders ceased. So did the gifts. And the fact that miracles are almost unknown in the Western church today served only to confirm their point of view.

As might be expected, many missionaries shared this interpretation of Scripture and settled for a dichotomy. The evangelists preached the gospel and saved souls while the doctors opened hospitals and healed bodies. In the eyes of the nationals there was no connection between the doctor with his lancet and the evangelist with his Bible. In this situation signs and wonders had no place; consequently the nationals were given a truncated version of the gospel.

We in the West equate religion with truth, forgetting that in the Third World the people equate religion with power. We ask, Is it true? They ask, Does it work? If it works, they want it; if it doesn't, they don't.

But all this is beginning to change. In recent years evangelicals are taking a second look at the role of signs and wonders as an evangelistic tool. Indeed, in Fuller Seminary School of World Mission they now have a course, taught by C. Peter Wagner, titled "Signs, Wonders, and Church Growth." Occasionally healing and other miracles take place right in the classroom. Needless to say, the course has attracted a good deal of attention on and off campus. Wagner believes that this is the beginning of a new era in world missions, when the power of the gospel will be presented along with the truth of the gospel. He is reported in *USA Today* as saying that "by the end of the century signs and wonders will be as common in American churches as Sunday school is today."

One large, well-known faith mission is presently coping with this very problem. It has appointed a task force to study the whole question and come up with a recommendation. Mission leaders are beginning to take seriously Paul's statement in Ephesians 6, where he reminds us that we wrestle not against flesh and blood but against demonic forces in the heavenlies. Several seminaries have recently introduced a new course titled "Power Encounter," among them Trinity Evangelical Divinity School and Columbia Graduate School of Bible and Missions. This is a most encouraging sign. It indicates that mission executives and seminary professors are getting back to the basics. For years we talked about apostolic methods and vied with one another to demonstrate their use, but we said little or nothing about apostolic power. We thought there was something magic about apostolic methods, and reasoned that if we could only employ them, we could win the world. Alas, we forgot that apostolic methods, without apostolic power, are no better than any other methods. Apostolic methods must be linked to apostolic power to achieve apostolic results. Our charismatic and Pentecostal friends have helped us immensely in this area and we owe them a debt of gratitude.

The Need for Revival

Another area that needs attention are the older churches in the Third World. The newer churches are doing well. In fact many of them are engaging in missionary work at home and overseas. But in many countries there are older churches—some of them several hundred years old—that are not doing so well. Most of them are found in the older parts of the mission field—India, Indonesia, Sri Lanka, and the Middle East—where Christianity was first introduced two or three hundred years ago.

With the passing of time, these churches lost their first love and have become old, stagnant, and moribund. They have long since ceased to evangelize their own countrymen. Indeed, they are losing church members to the indigenous religions. Some third- and fourth-generation Christians in India are reverting to Hinduism, and some church members in Sri Lanka are going back to Buddhism.

In chapter after chapter Johnstone in *Operation World* bemoans the fact that the older churches are dead and need to be revived. Not only have they lost their zeal, but they also have lapsed back into idolatry, immorality, witchcraft, and other practices prevalent in the non-Christian community. Such churches are not a good advertisement for the gospel; it goes without saying that they have no spiritual outreach in the community.

What should we do with these churches? Write them off and start all over again with new churches? Or should we seek to revive and renew these churches so that they too may play a part in the evangelization of the world? There is great potential in these churches—if only they can be revived. Certainly they should not be written off. Once revived and renewed they can become a powerful force in world evangelization.

And they *can* be revived! John Sung, the great Chinese revivalist, proved that when he visited Southeast Asia in the 1940s. Wherever he went, Chinese churches were revived, sinners were soundly converted, nominal church members, including leaders and pastors, came under conviction, confessed their sins, made restitution, and in their newfound zeal organized gospel teams that took the gospel message into the surrounding community.

Church revival is the surest way to church growth and the results often last for a generation. Many of the older church members in Southeast Asia still remember Sung and his meetings. The same is true of the East Africa revival of the 1930s. Bishop Festo Kivengere of Uganda, one of Africa's outstanding evangelists, is a product of that revival, and wherever he goes, he spreads revival. If these churches could be revived, they would do more for the evangelization of the world than would hundreds of Western missionaries.

This seems to be an area that we have largely overlooked. In so doing, I think we have made a mistake. Who knows what might happen if these churches all over the world were to be revived? At least, we should pray to that end. We do well to bear in mind that the modern missionary movement, the greatest in the history of the church, was the direct outcome of the revivals in Europe under the Pietists and the Moravians and the Evangelical Awakening in England under John Wesley.

East/West Cooperation

One thing more remains to be discussed. What should be the relationship between Western missions and the churches in the Third World?

A generation ago William Temple referred to the churches in the Third World as the "great new fact of our era." If that was true then, it is much truer now. These churches are much larger, stronger, and more numerous than they were in Temple's time. And they can no longer be ignored. The missions based in the West must devise some way of working in close cooperation with these churches.

Today the "great new fact" includes the missions in the Third World, not just the churches. With the collapse of the colonial system, many churches in the Third World have learned to stand on their own feet, pay their own way, and educate their own ministry. And they have done more. In the last 15 or 20 years they have begun to assume their responsibility for the evangelization of the world. This is one of the most significant, most exciting features of the modern missionary movement, which for almost two centuries depended on Western resources of men and money.

At the present time there are probably close to 20,000 non-Caucasian missionaries working in all six continents, and the number is increasing each year. Western mission agencies then must devise some way of coming to terms with this new phenomenon.

The colonial system is dead, but the colonial spirit is still very much alive, even in the minds of some missionaries. Jim Reapsome hit the nail on the head when he wrote, "For more than 200 years we have had the money and the power to do what we wanted to do anywhere in the world. We have been terribly slow to recognize that colonialism and paternalism in missions have died, and we should bury them." He goes on to say:

As Westerners, we're programmed to think that . . . we are the best, we know the most, and we can do it better. . . . Instead of barging into a country, setting up shop wherever we please, and doing our own thing, we could first sit down with our brothers and sisters and ask them where and how we could help them to do the job they think should be done. The initiative, leadership, and responsibility are theirs immediately. We are servants right from the start.[6]

This means that Western mission agencies must learn to cooperate with the missions as well as with the churches. To date not much thought has been given to this particular problem. However, progress is being made. The Chinese appear to be leading the way under the leadership of the Chinese Coordination Center for World Evangelism in Hong Kong. A seminar on Chinese and Western Leadership Cooperation was held in Hong Kong in September 1977. It was attended by 65 Chinese and 29 Westerners. Two position papers were "A Critique of Chinese and Western Cooperation in the Past" by Denis Lane, of Overseas Missionary Fellowship, Singapore, and "Possibilities and Opportunities of Cooperation in the Future," by Philip Teng, of the Christian and Missionary Alliance, Hong

6. *Evangelical Missions Quarterly*, October 1985, pp. 396–97.

Kong. To my knowledge this is the first seminar of its kind, and augurs well for the future.

Several things should be noted about this seminar:

1. It was the first of its kind.
2. It was convened by the Chinese, not the missionaries.
3. It was held on Chinese turf—Hong Kong.
4. The seminar was dominated by Chinese speakers.
5. There was excellent rapport between the missionaries and their Chinese counterparts, the missionaries acknowledging the mistakes of the past and the Chinese expressing their gratitude for what the missionaries had done to bring them the gospel.
6. A report of the seminar was published in Hong Kong under the title *Chinese and Western Leadership Cooperation Seminar Compendium*.

It is to be hoped that leaders in other Third World countries will get together with the missionaries to discuss policies and problems of mutual concern. The day is gone when the Western missionary could do his own thing, in his own way, with his own funds.

Today the traffic is moving in both directions: from West to East and from East to West. As church life and Christian values in the Western world continue to deteriorate, the need for outside help will increase in the days ahead. By the twenty-first century we may have to look to the Third World for pastors, as well as missionaries! Already we are hiring high-school teachers from Germany and Spain!

We are beginning to see movement in this direction. Some Western agencies have for the first time opened their membership to non-Caucasians. In the vanguard of this movement are the Overseas Missionary Fellowship, Sudan Interior Mission, Africa Inland Mission, BMMF International and others. The Latin America Mission went a good deal farther and was willing to lose its individual identity when it agreed to merge with several Latin American organizations to become the Community of Latin American Evangelical Ministries. Dennis E. Clark is not sure that Third World nationals have any great desire to be identified with Western organizations. "It seems almost too late," he says, "for Western societies to recruit the national because with very few exceptions the stigma of being labeled a 'stooge' or 'puppet' reduces usefulness. The more likely pattern of development will be the strengthening of existing missionary societies in Third World nations and proliferation of others."[7]

The Rise of Third World Leaders

Another encouraging development is the fact that outstanding leaders from the Third World are frequent speakers at world and regional conferences and seminars once dominated by Westerners. Included are John Richard, executive secretary of the Evangelical Fellowship of Asia; Tokunboh Adeyemo, executive secretary of the Association of Evangelical Churches of Africa and Madagascar; Philip Teng, chairman of the Christian and Missionary Alliance, Hong Kong; René Padilla, general secretary of the Latin American Theological Fraternity; Ro Bong-Rin, executive secretary of the Asia Theological Association; Andrew Furuyama, executive secretary of the Japan Overseas Missions Association; Gottfried Osei-Mensah of Ghana, first executive secretary of the Lausanne Committee for World Evangelization; Thomas Wang, secretary general of the Chinese Coordination Center for World Evangelism, Hong Kong; Saphir Athyal, president of Union Biblical Seminary, India; Samuel Escobar, president of the Latin American Theological Fraternity, Argentina; Paul Cho, pastor of the Yoido Full Gospel

---

7. Dennis E. Clark, *The Third World and Mission* (Waco: Word, 1971), p. 45.

Church, Seoul. And Luis Palau, of Argentina, is second only to Billy Graham as a world evangelist.

Another step in the right direction is the placing of Third World nationals in charge of Western-based organizations. When Stacey Woods stepped down as executive secretary of the International Fellowship of Evangelical Students, he was succeeded by Chau Wee Huan, a Chinese from Singapore. When Inter-Varsity Christian Fellowship wanted a new director in Canada, they chose Escobar from Latin America. When Hudson Taylor Armerding retired as president of the World Evangelical Fellowship, Theodore Williams of India succeeded him.

Financial Support for Third World Missions

One of the unsolved problems is how Western churches and missions can best help the emerging missionary agencies of the Third World.

It is not likely that many Western missionaries will elect to serve under other auspices when they have such a wide choice here in the West. If we cannot help with personnel, is it wise to help financially? Has the time come to think in global terms—one world, one church, one gospel, one mission? Dare we go on to say, one purse? Has the time come for us to combine all of our resources in East and West in men and money, to complete the job of world evangelization?

The greatest need in many parts of the Third World is finance. Many churches would like to engage in world missions, but are so poor that they do well to support a pastor at home, much less a missionary overseas. Then again, there are countries, such as India, where the government does not permit national churches to send money out of the country. If Indian missionaries are to serve overseas they must be supported by funds from outside India.

This is not a new idea. During World War II, when Adolph Hitler would not permit funds to be sent abroad, the International Missionary Council came to the rescue and used funds from British, American, and other churches to support German missionaries in all parts of the world. If this kind of thing proved beneficial in an emergency, why can't it be adopted as a regular practice? Another consideration is the soaring cost of missionary support. Indeed, one wonders if Western missions are not about to price themselves out of the market. To support a missionary family in Japan now costs $48,000 a year. I know of a couple with one small child that is hoping to leave shortly for Latin America. They list the following financial needs: personal budget, $1,625 per month; work budget, $1,572.30 per month; and outgoing expenses $12,500. And they are not going to Timbuktu but to Lima, Peru!

It is common knowledge that it costs, in some instances, ten times as much to support a missionary as to support a national worker. They are accustomed to a much simpler lifestyle; consequently they can live comfortably on a much smaller budget.

As a result, some churches in the West are taking a second look at their missionary budget and wondering if they are getting a good return on their money. Consequently, some churches are looking for nationals to support, and some organizations are specializing in this approach. However, there are real dangers. In spite of good intentions, too much money given to national churches and workers may, in the long run, do more harm than good. Besides, a national worker, supported by Western funds, may easily become suspect in his own community.

Christian Nationals Evangelism Commission, based in California, is engaged in this kind of operation. To avoid the aforementioned pitfalls, there is close cooperation, adequate supervision, and strict accountability.

Is this the wave of the future? Has the time come for a new look at world missions? Are we in the West prepared to recognize that the church universal is one; therefore the world mission should also be one? It is an intriguing idea and one that deserves close scrutiny.

As we approach the twenty-first century we can derive some comfort from the fact that we are moving in the right direction, and the momentum seems to be on the increase. When will we be able to complete the task? When every pastor, in East or West, can say with Wesley, "The world is my parish"; and when every church member, with Frances Ridley Havergal, can say:

> Take my life and let it be
> Consecrated, Lord, to Thee.

And every young Christian can say:

> Take my feet and let them move
> At the impulse of Thy love.

And every Christian businessman can say:

> Take my silver and my gold,
> Not a mite would I withhold.

Select Bibliography

Adeney, Miriam. *God's Foreign Policy*. Grand Rapids: Eerdmans, 1984.

Anderson, Gerald H., ed. *Witnessing to the Kingdom: Melbourne and Beyond*. Maryknoll, N.Y.: Orbis, 1982.

Anderson, Gerald H., and Thomas F. Stransky, eds. *Christ's Lordship and Religious Pluralism*. Maryknoll, N.Y.: Orbis, 1981.

Anderson, Norman. *Christianity and World Religions: The Challenge of Pluralism*. Rev. ed. Downers Grove: InterVarsity, 1984.

Barrett, David B., ed. *World Christian Encyclopedia*. New York: Oxford University Press, 1982.

Bauer, Arthur, O. F. *Making Mission Happen*. New York: Friendship, 1974.

Beaver, R. Pierce. *American Protestant Women in World Mission: A History of the First Feminist Movement in North America*. Rev. ed. Grand Rapids: Eerdmans, 1980.

Bliss, David. *Student Mission Power: Student Volunteer Movement*. Pasadena: William Carey Library, 1979.

Boer, Harry R. *Pentecost and Missions*. Grand Rapids: Eerdmans, 1961.

Bosch, David J. *Witness to the World: The Christian Mission in Theological Perspective*. Atlanta: John Knox, 1980.

Brierley, Peter, ed. *UK Christian Handbook, 1984*. London: Evangelical Alliance, 1984.

Bryant, David. *In the Gap: What It Means to Be a World Christian*. Downers Grove: InterVarsity, 1979.

Buhlmann, Walbert. *The Coming of the Third Church: An Analysis of the Present and Future of the Church.* Maryknoll, N.Y.: Orbis, 1977.

Burney, James E. *You Can Tell the World.* Downers Grove: InterVarsity, 1979.

Chaney, Charles L. *The Birth of Missions in America.* Pasadena: William Carey Library, 1976.

Chinese and Western Leadership Cooperation Seminar Compendium. Hong Kong: Chinese Coordination Center of World Evangelism, 1980.

Cho, David J. *New Forces in Missions.* Seoul: East-West Center for Mission Research and Development, 1976.

Clark, Dennis E. *The Third World and Mission.* Waco: Word, 1971.

Coggins, Wade T. *So That's What Missions Is All About.* Chicago: Moody, 1975.

Coggins, Wade T., and Edwin L. Frizen, Jr., eds. *Christ and Caesar in Christian Missions.* Pasadena: William Carey Library, 1979.

_____, eds. *Reaching Our Generation.* Pasadena: William Carey Library, 1982.

Collins, Marjorie A. *Manual for Accepted Missionary Candidates.* Pasadena: William Carey Library, 1972.

Costas, Orlando E. *Christ Outside the Gate: Mission Beyond Christendom.* Maryknoll, N.Y.: Orbis, 1982.

_____. *The Church and Its Mission: A Shattering Critique from the Third World.* Wheaton: Tyndale, 1975; San Francisco: Harper and Row, 1979.

Dayton, Edward R. and David A. Fraser. *Planning Strategies for World Evangelization.* Grand Rapids: Eerdmans, 1980.

Dayton, Edward R., and Samuel Wilson, eds. *The Future of World Evangelization: Unreached Peoples '84.* Monrovia, Calif.: MARC, 1984.

Detzler, Wayne A. *The Changing Church in Europe: Religious Movements Since 1960.* Grand Rapids: Zondervan, 1978.

Dowsett, Dick. *God, That's Not Fair.* Robesonia, Penn.: OMF, 1982.

Dubose, Francis M. *God Who Sends: A Fresh Quest for Biblical Mission.* Nashville: Broadman, 1983.

Durant, Will. *Caesar and Christ: A History of Roman Civilization from Its Beginnings to A.D. 337.* New York: Simon and Schuster, 1944.

Engstrom, Ted W. *What in the World Is God Doing? The New Face of Missions.* Waco: Word, 1978.

Escobar, Samuel, and John Driver. *Christian Mission and Social Justice*. Scottdale, Penn.: Herald, 1978.

Falk, Peter. *The Growth of the Church in Africa*. Grand Rapids: Zondervan, 1979.

Fenton, Horace L., Jr. *Myths about Missions*. Downers Grove: InterVarsity, 1973.

Fife, Eric S., and Arthur F. Glasser. *Missions in Crisis: Rethinking Missionary Strategy*. Chicago: InterVarsity, 1961.

Flanagan, Padraig, ed. *A New Missionary Era*. Maryknoll, N.Y.: Orbis, 1979.

Glasser, Arthur F., and Donald A. McGavran. *Contemporary Theologies of Mission*. Grand Rapids: Baker, 1983.

Glover, Robert H. *The Bible Basis of Missions*. Chicago: Moody, 1964.

Goddard, Burton L., ed. *The Encyclopedia of Modern Christian Missions: The Agencies*. Camden, N.J.: Nelson, 1967.

Griffiths, Michael. *The Church and World Mission*. Grand Rapids: Zondervan, 1980.

_____. *Give Up Your Small Ambitions*. London: InterVarsity, 1970.

Hancock, Robert L., ed. *The Ministry of Development in Evangelical Perspective: A Symposium on the Social and Spiritual Mandate*. Pasadena: William Carey Library, 1979.

Hanks, Thomas D. *God So Loved the Third World: The Bible, the Reformation, and Liberation Theologies*. Translated by James C. Dekker. Maryknoll, N.Y.: Orbis, 1983.

Hastings, Adrian. *A History of African Christianity, 1950–1975*. Cambridge: Cambridge University Press, 1979.

Hedlund, Roger E., ed. *World Christianity: South Asia*. Monrovia, Calif.: MARC, 1980.

Henderson, W. Guy. *Passport to Missions*. Nashville: Broadman, 1979.

Hesselgrave, David J. *Communicating Christ Cross-Culturally*. Grand Rapids: Zondervan, 1978.

_____. *Planting Churches Cross-Culturally: A Guide for Home and Foreign Missions*. Grand Rapids: Baker, 1980.

_____, ed. *New Horizons in World Mission: Evangelicals and the Christian Mission in the 1980s*. Grand Rapids: Baker, 1979.

Hillis, Don W. *Missions Today: A New Challenge*. Chicago: Moody, 1975.

Hitt, Russell T. *Cannibal Valley*. New York: Harper and Row, 1962; Harrisburg, Penn.: Christian Publications, 1981.

Hoke, Donald E., ed. *The Church in Asia*. Chicago: Moody, 1975.

Holland, Clifton L., ed. *World Christianity: Central America and the Caribbean*. Monrovia, Calif.: MARC, 1981.

Hopkins, Paul A. *What Next in Mission?* Philadelphia: Westminster, 1977.

Howard, David M. *The Great Commission for Today*. Downers Grove: InterVarsity, 1976.

———. *Student Power in World Evangelism*. Downers Grove: InterVarsity, 1970.

Hulbert, Terry C. *World Missions Today*. Wheaton: Evangelical Teacher Training Association, 1982.

Inch, Morris. *Doing Theology Across Cultures*. Grand Rapids: Baker, 1982.

Jacobs, Donald R. *Pilgrimage in Mission*. Scottdale, Penn.: Herald, 1983.

Johnstone, Patrick J. *Operation World: A Handbook for World Intercession*. Bromley, England: STL Publications, 1980.

Lindsell, Harold, ed. *The Church's Worldwide Mission*. Waco: Word, 1966.

Kane, J. Herbert. *The Christian World Mission: Today and Tomorrow*. Grand Rapids: Baker, 1981.

———. *A Concise History of the Christian World Mission*. Rev. ed. Grand Rapids: Baker, 1982.

———. *Understanding Christian Missions*. Rev. ed. Grand Rapids: Baker, 1986.

Kennedy, Betty Jo. *The Missionary Family*. Pasadena: William Carey Library, 1983.

Keyes, Lawrence E. *The Last Age of Missions: A Study of Third World Mission Societies*. Pasadena: William Carey Library, 1982.

Kohls, L. Robert. *Survival Kit for Overseas Living*. Chicago: Intercultural Press, 1979.

Kyle, John E., ed. *The Unfinished Task: A Tribute to the Haystack Prayer Meeting and the Modern Missionary Movement*. Ventura, Calif.: Regal, 1984.

Latourette, Kenneth Scott. *Christianity Through the Ages*. New York: Harper and Row, 1965.

Law, Gail. *Chinese Churches Handbook.* Hong Kong: Chinese Coordination Center for World Evangelism, 1982.

Liao, David C., ed. *World Christianity: Eastern Asia.* Monrovia, Calif.: MARC, 1979.

Lockerbie, Jeannie. *By Ones and by Twos: Single and Double Missionaries.* Pasadena: William Carey Library, 1983.

Lyall, Leslie. *God Reigns in China.* Robesonia, Penn.: OMF, 1985.

McCurry, Don M., ed. *The Gospel and Islam: A 1978 Compendium.* Monrovia, Calif.: MARC, 1979.

_____, ed. *World Christianity: Middle East.* Monrovia, Calif.: MARC, 1979.

McGavran, Donald A. *Momentous Decisions in Missions Today.* Grand Rapids: Baker, 1984.

McQuilkin, Robertson. *The Great Omission.* Grand Rapids: Baker, 1984.

Murray, Andrew. *Key to the Missionary Problem.* Fort Washington, Penn.: Christian Literature Crusade, 1979.

Neill, Stephen. *Call to Mission.* Philadelphia: Fortress, 1970.

_____. *A History of Christian Missions.* New York: Penguin, 1964.

_____. *The Unfinished Task.* London: Edinburgh House, 1957.

Neill, Stephen, Gerald H. Anderson, and John Goodwin, eds. *Concise Dictionary of the Christian World Mission.* London: Lutterworth, 1970.

Nelson, Marlin L. *The How and Why of Third World Missions: An Asian Case Study.* Pasadena: William Carey Library, 1976.

Nelson, Wilton M. *Protestantism in Central America.* Grand Rapids: Eerdmans, 1984.

Newell, William J., ed. *Reaching Canada's Unreached.* Monrovia, Calif.: MARC, 1983.

Parshall, Phil. *Beyond the Mosque: Christians Within Muslim Community.* Grand Rapids: Baker, 1985.

_____. *Bridges to Islam: A Christian Perspective on Folk Islam.* Grand Rapids: Baker, 1983.

_____. *New Paths in Muslim Evangelism: Evangelical Approaches to Contextualization.* Grand Rapids: Baker, 1980.

Parvin, Earl. *Mission USA.* Chicago: Moody, 1985.

Pentecost, Edward. *Issues in Missiology: An Introduction.* Grand Rapids: Baker, 1982.

Preheim, Marion K. *Overseas Service Manual.* Scottdale, Penn.: Herald, 1969.

Reed, Lyman E. *Preparing Missionaries for Intercultural Communication.* Pasadena: William Carey Library, 1985.

Richardson, Don. *Eternity in Their Hearts.* Ventura, Calif.: Regal, 1981.

Ro, Bong-Rin. *The Bible and Theology in Asian Contexts.* Taipei: Asian Theological Association, 1984.

———. *Voice of the Church in Asia.* Hong Kong: Christian Communications, 1975.

Ro, Bong-Rin, and Marlin L. Nelson. *Korean Church Growth Explosion.* Seoul: Word of Life Press, 1983.

Rossi, Sanna Barlow. *God's City in the Jungle.* Wheaton: Tyndale, 1975.

Scherer, James A. *Global Living Here and Now.* New York: Friendship, 1974.

———, ed. *Missionary, Go Home! A Reappraisal of the Christian World Mission.* Englewood Cliffs, N.J.: Prentice-Hall, 1964.

Schindler, Robert, and Marian Schindler. *Mission Possible: World Missions in the 1980s.* Wheaton: Victor, 1983.

Scott, Waldron. *Serving Our Generation: Evangelical Strategies for the Eighties.* Colorado Springs, Colo.: World Evangelical Fellowship, 1980.

Shenk, Wilbert R. *Anabaptism and Mission.* Scottdale, Penn.: Herald, 1984.

———. *Exploring Church Growth.* Grand Rapids: Eerdmans, 1983.

———, ed. *Mission Focus: Current Issues.* Scottdale, Penn.: Herald, 1980.

Sider, Ronald J. *Rich Christians in an Age of Hunger: A Biblical Study.* Downers Grove: InterVarsity, 1977.

Sine, Tom. *The Mustard Seed Conspiracy: You Can Make a Difference in Tomorrow's Troubled World.* Waco: Word, 1981.

Skoglund, John E. *To the Whole Creation: The Church Is Mission.* Valley Forge, Penn.: Judson, 1962.

Starkes, M. Thomas. *God's Commissioned People.* Nashville: Broadman, 1984.

Stott, John R. W. *Christian Mission in the Modern World.* Downers Grove: InterVarsity, 1975.

Taber, Charles R., ed. *The Church in Africa, 1977*. Pasadena: William Carey Library, 1978.

Trueblood, Elton. *The Validity of the Christian Mission*. New York: Harper and Row, 1972.

Tucker, Ruth. *From Jerusalem to Irian Jaya: A Biographical History of Christian Missions*. Grand Rapids: Zondervan, 1983.

Tuggy, Joy T. *The Missionary Wife and Her Work*. Chicago: Moody, 1966.

Wagner, C. Peter. *Frontiers in Missionary Strategy*. Chicago: Moody, 1972.

_____. *Look Out! The Pentecostals Are Coming*. Carol Stream, Ill.: Creation House, 1973.

_____. *On the Crest of the Wave: Becoming a World Christian*. Ventura, Calif.: Regal, 1983.

_____. *Stop the World, I Want to Get On*. Pasadena: William Carey Library, 1973.

Wakatama, Pius. *Independence for the Third World Church: An African's Perspective on Missionary Work*. Downers Grove: InterVarsity, 1976.

Wallis, Jim. *The Call to Conversion: Recovering the Gospel for These Times*. New York: Harper and Row, 1981.

Warren, Max A. *I Believe in the Great Commission*. Grand Rapids: Eerdmans, 1976.

Webster, Douglas. *Yes to Mission*. New York: Seabury, 1966.

White, John. *The Golden Cow: Materialism in the Twentieth-Century Church*. Downers Grove: InterVarsity, 1979.

Wicks, Doug, ed. *Forget the Pith Helmet: Perspectives on the Missionary Experience*. Chicago: Moody, 1984.

Wilson, J. Christy, Jr. *Today's Tentmakers: Self-Support: An Alternative Model for Worldwide Witness*. Wheaton: Tyndale, 1979.

Wilson, Samuel, ed. *Mission Handbook: North American Protestant Ministries Overseas*. 12th ed. Monrovia, Calif.: MARC, 1980.

Winter, Ralph D. *The Twenty-Five Unbelievable Years, 1945–1969*. Pasadena: William Carey Library, 1970.

Winter, Ralph D., and Steven C. Hawthorne, eds. *Perspectives on the World Christian Movement: A Reader*. Pasadena: William Carey Library, 1981.

Wong, Peter, ed. *Missions from the Third World: A World Survey of Non-Western Missions in Asia, Africa, and Latin America*. Singapore: Church Growth Center, 1973.

Subject Index

Abdul-Haqq, Akbar, 20
Adeney, David, 22
Adeyemo, Tokunboh, 221
Afghanistan, 127
Africa, 98, 123–24, 210; church
  revival in, 217; nationalism in,
  121; political conditions in, 48–49,
  50; theological education in,
  101–2. *See also* Black Africa;
  specific country
Africa Inland Mission, 220
Africa Now, 172
African Christian Students
  Fellowship, 36
All-Filipino Congress on
  Evangelism, 22–23
America. *See* United States of
  America
American Bible Society, 95, 172
American Coptic Association, 128
Anglican Church, 25, 50, 97
Angola, 33, 132
Animism, 19, 118
Apostasy, Law of, 104, 119
Apostle(s), 84; mission of, 85–86,
  115–16, 142–43; persecution of,
  125–26
Appenzeller, Henry, 20
Armerding, Hudson Taylor, 222
Asia, 99; church growth in, 157–58;
  church revival in, 217; evangelical
  tasks in, 103, 210; opposition to
  missionaries in, 118–19; political

conditions in, 49, 50; poverty in,
  45; prejudice in, 120; social impact
  of missionaries in, 111. *See also*
  specific country
Asia Evangelical Fellowship, 35
Asia Theological Association, 221
Assemblies of God, 20, 47, 100, 172
Association of Evangelical Churches
  of Africa and Madagascar, 100,
  221
Athyal, Saphir, 221
Augsburger, Myron, 19
Azariah (bishop), 105

Bandung Conference, 39
Bangladesh, 31, 45
Baptist Church, 26, 34, 97, 159,
  210–11
Barzini, Luigi, 145
Batak Church, 47–48
Bhutan, 27
Bible Basis of Missions, The
  (Glover), 212 nn. 1, 2
Bible colleges, 173. *See also*
  Theological education
Bible correspondence courses, 19,
  30–31, 96
Bible distribution, 28, 33–34, 91,
  94–96, 99
Bibles for the World, Inc., 91
Bible-study groups, 23
Bible translation, 32–33, 50
Bitterman, Chet, 51

233

Qadhafi, Muammar, 126

Racial prejudice, 119–20
Radio broadcasting, 19, 26, 28–30,
    31, 95
Radio Moscow, 29
Rajastan Gospel Mission, 28
Readings in Third World Missions
    (Nelson), 38
Reagan, Ronald, 127
Reapsome, Jim, 219
Redemption, 67–69, 80, 90, 138
Religious fanaticism, 117–19
Religious freedom, restrictions on,
    127–28
Religious Knowledge, in public
    schools, 31–32, 198
Resurrection, 85–86
Revival, of older churches, 216–18
Richard, John, 221
Richardson, Don, 91
*Rich Christians in an Age of
    Hunger: Revised and Expanded*
    (Sider), 193, 194
Ro, Bong-Rin, 221
Roberts, Oral, 156
Roman Catholic Church, 18, 20, 24,
    50, 103–4, 129, 208, 214;
    missionary activities of, 20, 103–4
Romulo, Carlos, 151
Rossi, Sanna Barlow, 91
Rule of God, 66–67, 71, 72

Salaries, of pastors, 98
Salvation: definition of, 89; personal,
    89–90, 91; societal, 90–91
Samuel, Vinay, 35
Satan, 55–59, 67, 88, 89
Scherer, James A., 193
Schuller, Robert, 156
Second Coming, 130, 141
Second World, 39
Segregation, 143–44
Seminary(ies), 35, 101–2, 173, 221.
    See also Theological education
Separatist churches, 24
Seventh-day Adventists, 35
Shah of Iran, 126
Shenouda III (pope), 128

Sider, Ronald J., 193, 194 n
Signs and wonders, 214–16
Sikkim, 27–28
SIM International, 98
Sin, 66–67, 88, 89, 140
Sine, Tom, 193
Singapore, 97
Single missionaries, 129–30
Skoglund, John E., 144, 144 n, 213
Social change, 111–12
Society, transformation of, 90–92
Sojourners, 189
Somalia, 157
Sorensen (Moravian missionary),
    207, 209
South Africa, 28, 157
Southern Baptist Convention, 210
Southern Baptists, 159
Speer, Robert E., 77, 78 n
Sri Lanka, 216, 217
Stewardship, accountability for,
    164–66
Stewart, James S., 145, 145 n
Strom, Donna, 91
Student groups, 12, 35–36, 130–31,
    199, 222
Sturz, Richard, 26
Sudan Interior Mission, 36, 220
Sunday, Billy, 169
Sung, John, 217
Support, missionary, 86–87, 222–24;
    by churches, 174–75; by
    individuals, 171–74

Taiwan, 97, 99, 106. *See also* China
Talents, sharing of, 168–69
Tanzania, 97
Teachers Abroad Program, 210
Teen Missions, 12
Television broadcasting, 30, 95
Temple, William, 218
Teng, Philip, 219, 221
Tentmaker missionaries, 127,
    197–200, 208–9
Tertullian, 72
Thailand, 18, 50–51, 121–22
Theological education, 99–102, 147,
    173, 216, 221

Scripture Index

243